Dear Julie,

Pray for peace

Live for love

Be nice to other

Best

Jeun

The Numbers on My
Parents'
Arms

★ ★ ★

Jerry Bagel

THE NUMBERS ON MY PARENTS' ARMS

iUniverse books may be ordered through booksellers or by contacting:

iUniverse
1663 Liberty Drive
Bloomington, IN 47403
www.iuniverse.com
1-800-Authors (1-800-288-4677)

ISBN: 978-1-5320-7968-9 (sc)
ISBN: 978-1-5320-7969-6 (hc)
ISBN: 978-1-5320-7967-2 (e)

Library of Congress Control Number: 2019912413

Print information available on the last page.

iUniverse rev. date: 09/23/2019

INTRODUCTION

I knew my mother and father were different from the other adults in the neighborhood by the time I was old enough to count. While the other kids learned their numbers through songs and books, I learned them by tracing my fingertip over the five-digit tattoos inked on my parents' left forearms.

I have vivid memories of childhood bedtimes, my father, Sam, lying beside me on top of my quilt.

"This one?" I'd ask, touching an indigo eight.

"Acht," he'd answer. Eight in Yiddish, my parents' preferred language and the one spoken in our home.

"And this?" I'd ask, tracing another squiggly mark.

"Finef," he'd answer. Five.

By the time I entered kindergarten, I could correctly identify the numbers on both of my parents' arms.

Mom's was 26069.

Dad's was 83935.

I had never heard the word *Holocaust*. There was no such word in the Yiddish language. Yet almost as far back as I can remember, growing up on a chicken farm in East Windsor, New Jersey, my parents spoke daily about the terrible things that had happened to them in *die lager*, the camps.

One night after our numerical exercises, it occurred to me that Dad probably hadn't been born with numbers on his arm. I asked him how he got them.

"In a place called Auschwitz," he answered.

The word sounded strange and harsh. "Was it bad there?" I asked.

"It was the worst place in the world."

This statement brought an abrupt end to the counting and marked the beginning of my formal education of the brutal histories of my parents. Like most children, I was hungry for every nugget of information they could share about the family I should have had—the grandparents, aunts, uncles, and dozens of cousins. The more I learned, the more questions I had.

Mom and Dad's horrible tales defied belief, though I knew they were true. While other kids fell asleep to stories about bunnies and trains, my parents were telling me almost everything about what their lives had been like in Poland. My bedtime stories contained all the fantastical elements of the most frightening fairy tales. Like in *Hansel and Gretel*, an evil entity was attempting to lure innocent children into a scorching red oven. But my parents' tales weren't mere words in a book, ending the way a child's last words before bed *should* end—with a happy ending and a good night kiss. The characters in my parents' stories *did* end up in the oven. And even more terrifying, they were my family.

My parents were Szlama and Chaja (later Sam and Helen when they arrived in the United States). The events in this book are all true. Where there were holes in my parents' stories, I was able to fill in the details by listening to and reading testimonies and memoirs of survivors who were in the same place at the same time as Sam and Helen. The United States Holocaust Memorial Museum in Washington, DC, was especially helpful in gathering every piece of documentation of my parents' time in the various camps. The Nazis were meticulous record keepers, and luckily, many of those pertaining to my father, who had a far bigger paper trail than my mother, weren't destroyed. Unfortunately, the Nazis were successful in destroying my mother's records.

Bethanne Kafasis, at the small but nonetheless mighty Cranbury Public Library in Cranbury, New Jersey, obtained by interlibrary loan many volumes of rare books to further help in my research.

I have given some political and military background to Sam and Helen's Holocaust experiences just to give context to where they were and what was happening to them. These events have been merely touched upon and can be subjects for further research if the reader desires.

ONE

In Plonsk, Poland, approximately sixty kilometers northwest of Warsaw, the number of Jews and non-Jews was virtually equal in the ten-thousand-person population. The goyim (Yiddish for non-Jews) lived in the surrounding countryside, and the Jews resided within the city center. Although the two groups had daily contact in the streets, markets, and shops, they never mixed socially.[1] The ethnic equity, however, helped to control the rampant anti-Semitism in other areas of Poland.

Jews had lived in Plonsk since 1446.[2] The town was an important center of Zionism, a term coined in 1890 for the movement seeking the return of the Jews to Palestine. The term comes from a reference to Mount Zion, one of the hills of Jerusalem.[3]

David Ben-Gurion (formerly Grün), who became the first prime minister of Israel, was born in Plonsk in 1886. Recalling his youth in the town, Ben-Gurion later wrote, "For many of us, anti-Semitic feeling had little to do with our dedication to Zionism. I personally never suffered anti-Semitic persecution. Plonsk was remarkably free of it ... Nevertheless, and I think this very significant, it was Plonsk that sent the highest proportion of Jews to Eretz Israel (land of Israel) from any town in Poland of comparable size. We emigrated not for negative reasons of escape but for the positive purpose of rebuilding a homeland."[4]

By 1906, Ben-Gurion, at twenty years of age, had left Plonsk and was living in Palestine, where he was instrumental in creating the first agricultural workers' commune, the *kvutzah* (common term for kibbutz before Israeli statehood, generally smaller in size).[5]

The above quote referred to a period that took place a generation before Szlama had been born. Unfortunately, Plonsk was not "remarkably free" of anti-Semitism a generation later, though it remained an important center of Zionism, especially for a town of its size.

Szlama's parents, Yosef and Devorah (née Fuks) Baijgel, had seven sons: Cheel, Yankel, Szlama, Itchele, Avraham Mendel, Freuim, and Srull Moshe. The family lived in a three-room wooden house on Varsha Gasse (Warsaw Street), a main road that led southeast to the capital city. The property consisted of a little house with a sheet metal roof, an outside privy, and a small stable, all surrounded by a stake fence.

Yosef had a short, pointed, well-trimmed beard and stood only five feet, two inches tall. His nickname was Yossel Eifella (Joseph the Dwarf), more a statement of fact than a disparagement.

Yosef made his living as a *kurnik* (poultry dealer), selling fowl for profit to both kosher and nonkosher butchers. It was an arduous way to make a living. Mondays through Thursdays, accompanied by a helper, he traveled in a horse-drawn wagon pulled to farms as far as thirty miles away. Visiting the farthest farms necessitated leaving home the night before. The markets opened early, and Yosef needed to buy from at least two or three farms to collect approximately two hundred birds. After getting them in their cages atop his wagon, he'd be at the *yareeds* (town squares) in Ciechanów, Warsaw, Płock, and Nowy Dwór, ready to sell when the markets first opened.

Tuesdays found Yosef at the yareed in Plonsk. There was a saying in Yiddish: "Dinstag iz ein mazldik tog." (Tuesday is a lucky day.) It was when the women of the town replenished the larder, haggled over prices, and visited with neighbors.

Yosef was successful enough to own his home outright. As a landowner, he was considered prosperous, which sparked both esteem and envy from his neighbors. Although not wealthy, Yosef had a position of respect in the town, and he was considered a wise man whose reputation spread beyond Plonsk's borders. People came from all over to discuss their disputes over contracts, property, damages, and insults, perceived or otherwise. He was known for his fair judgment.

Yosef had high standards for his children as well. He was a strict disciplinarian who didn't flinch from administering a leather strap to the backsides of his boys if he felt their actions necessitated it.

Devorah was a devoted wife and mother, as well as an excellent cook, who worked hard to keep her large family well fed. Every Friday night after Shabbat (Sabbath) services, she would present a table crowded with dishes. In the summer, when fresh beets were in season, bright, magenta-colored borscht served with freshly dug, boiled potatoes, sour cream, and dill from her garden adorned the table. Most meals began with gefilte fish made from live carp purchased that week at the market. In the colder months, there'd be cabbage soup or the hallmark of every respectable Jewish homemaker, golden chicken soup with kreplach, dumplings stuffed with meat or mashed potato. This was often followed by *katchka* (roast duck) and baked potatoes. Another favorite was Devorah's stuffed cabbage leaves, bursting with a ground-meat-and-rice mixture, bathed in a tangy tomato sauce and sprinkled with sweet, fat raisins to balance the flavor.

Shabbat dinner often ended with jam-filled blintzes or honey cake and hot tea. Sweet dessert wine and singing added warmth to the frigid evenings of the harsh winters in Poland.

Like most Jewish Plonskers, the Baijgel family lived close to the town center, with its multistory brick buildings, and separately from the more recently arrived goyim, who tended to settle in the outskirts of town.

Times were relatively good for the Jewish Plonskers during Szlama's youth. Poland was a state created by the Allied powers after winning the Great War in 1919, the year Szlama turned six. The country was recreated from parts of the defunct German, Austro-Hungarian, and Russian empires. The new Polish Republic was a melting pot of ethnic minority groups, including Germans, Ukrainians, Lithuanians, Slovaks, and roughly three million Jews. Polish authorities agreed to protect the civil rights of these non-Polish minorities by signing the so-called Little Treaty of Versailles (also known as the Minorities Treaty) on June 28, 1919.[6]

Marshal Jozef Piłsudski was in charge. He was not anti-Semitic and did not tolerate it among his followers. Most Jews in Poland knew the fable of Piłsudski, who, while commanding the Polish army during the Polish-Soviet War in 1920, was hidden under the dress of a Jewish woman when the Russians came looking for him. It was thought to be the reason he had an affinity for the Jewish people. True or not, he quelled the waves of populist anti-Semitism while he was in office during Szlama's childhood.

As a boy, Szlama certainly could not imagine the horrific events that lay ahead. They would have seemed inconceivable to anyone living in Plonsk between the two world wars. One of his happiest childhood memories illustrates how much contentment the simple pleasures of small-town life brought him: sitting under a tree at the age of eight, enjoying the light breeze, while his faithful dog, Figger, licked his bare toes, and pondering that being eighty years old was a long time away. He saw his future as a chain of such simple, rustic moments.

Like many Polish boys, Szlama's great passion was football (soccer). He played right wing for a team in the town's Jewish League. The goyim had their own league. But if their club was in the city finals and needed strong players to boost their chances of winning, they had no qualms about drafting talented Jewish boys to augment their team. Szlama was a strong-enough player to have participated in several such championship games. During the winters, when the lakes froze, he played informal pickup ice hockey games, intermingling with the town's goyim on the ice. For skates, Szlama strapped blades onto his shoes. The games were rough enough that players occasionally lost a few teeth.

As he got older, Szlama also had close contact with goyim boys in Plonsk's pool halls. There was always an underlying tension between the two groups, the Jews against the Shaguzem (Yiddish plural for gentile males, a counterpart to Shiksas, gentile females). Occasionally, verbal quarrels erupted into brawls, and the cue sticks became weapons. But the goyim were wary of the Jews because their families' and friends' homes were concentrated near the city center. Goyim reinforcements were farther away, on the outskirts of the town and in the countryside. Szlama and his friends could quickly call for backup if a truly serious fight broke out.

In this quasi-tolerant atmosphere, Szlama's childhood was relatively free of strife. He walked to heder (Jewish elementary school that taught basic Judaism and Hebrew) three or four times a week and slowly progressed with his Hebrew lessons in preparation for becoming a Bar Mitzvah.

Yosef felt that the heder's program was not rigorous enough for Szlama, so he hired an elderly rabbi to come to the house each week to test his progress. The old rabbi would stroke his long white beard and lean over Szlama's shoulder while Yosef stood intently watching nearby. If Szlama failed to demonstrate adequate progress in his weekly lessons, the leather strap came out and there'd be hell to pay, so he made sure to perfect his Hebrew. When Szlama turned thirteen, Yosef took him to shul (temple), and Szlama, wearing a new blue suit, received an *Aliyah* (Hebrew word for the honor of being called upon to read from the Torah, the scroll containing the law of God as revealed to Moses and recorded in the first five books of the Hebrew scriptures). After the ceremony, a *kiddish* (celebratory meal after synagogue) consisting of sponge cake and wine was served. There was none of the lavish partying associated with the Bar Mitzvahs of today. Despite the modest celebration, the money Yosef spent on Szlama's new suit was a testament to how important the ancient ritual was to Yosef.

Most of the Jewish youth in Plonsk belonged to one of the town's many Zionist youth groups. At the height of their activity, the youth movements in Plonsk had hundreds of members, Szlama being one of them. Most of the groups had clubs and libraries, as well as groups for sports, drama, drills, and self-defense, some of which were held on the city's football pitch. The youth groups also held activities and lectures, political gatherings, conferences, trips, scout camps, and summer camps.[7] The youth group activities influenced many Jews in Plonsk, including young Szlama, to consider immigrating to Israel. Szlama was a committed Zionist who maintained a lifelong devotion to Israel and Israeli causes.

Dwarfed in size by the Zionist movement was the illegal Communist Party. Plonsk counted many Jews amongst its members, and plenty of them were arrested and indicted for Communist activity. Rallies could get heated, with parading members chanting the following:

> Shmeer da guilloteeno, shmeer da guilloteeno,
> shmeer da guilloteeno mit facista blut;
> Blut mus fliggen;
> Forverd nish zurrick;
> Vir guyen und mir camfin fur da rotte republik!

> Smear the guillotine; smear the guillotine, smear
> the guillotine;
> Blood must fly;
> Forward not backward;
> We are going and we are fighting for the Red
> Republic!

When he wasn't studying the Torah or playing football, Szlama enjoyed hiking with Figger to a creek in the pine forests that bordered the town. He fished for pike and perch and secretly snacked on black pumpernickel spread with *chaser fleisch* (Yiddish for lard). To consume *treif* (nonkosher food, such as pork and shellfish) was to turn one's back on the laws of the Torah. If Yosef had found out, Szlama would have gotten the beating of his life.

Poultry was a mainstay of the kosher diet, giving Yosef a more-than-modest business. He bought chickens, turkeys, geese, and ducks from goyim farmers of all socioeconomic backgrounds. Some of his suppliers were wealthy landowners whose property was vast enough to employ tenant workers; others had small parcels of land run by single struggling families. Yosef treated them all equally, paying fair prices for their birds. When Szlama was available, he worked beside his father to learn the family business.

Unfortunately, Szlama's relatively idyllic family life ended when he was thirteen. His mother died at only thirty-eight years old. Ever practical, Yosef quickly remarried a younger woman to help raise his boys. Within a year, a new baby girl joined the family.

Later, Yosef explained to his sons, "I wanted her to be pregnant so she wouldn't run away."

Clearly, he had understood how difficult caring for seven grieving boys would be for his new wife. To add to her burdens, a second baby girl soon arrived.

Although Szlama had a warm relationship with his stepmother and would help care for her until her deportation at the end of 1942, he was emotionally battered by the loss of his mother. He began having trouble concentrating on his schoolwork and eventually dropped out to go to work after finishing fifth grade, augmenting the family income. There were eleven mouths to feed. His choice of trade was clear. He became a kurnik, like his father, and built his own hand-pulled, two-story, three-by-two-feet poultry cart that could hold up to sixteen chickens. He paid a blacksmith to rim the wooden wheels with tin so they wouldn't crack on the rough bricks and cobblestones.

Szlama's new life was hard. He rose before dawn and worked until evening six days a week, with Saturdays off for the Sabbath. But he had a good, solid cart and developed strong legs from the physical labor. Although he was short like his father and thin, his arms became muscular, and he learned to lift and sling heavy poultry cages onto the bed of the cart and stack them over his head. Soon he could load two large crates, each holding sixteen birds. Some days, he bought turkeys and carried them in double cages. Other days, he had crates with as many as six ducks or three geese each. Like his father, he did business with Jewish and goyim butchers.

The contact he had with goyim farm boys gave him a perspective on life in nearby market towns such as Nowy Dwor Mazowiecki, which were alien worlds to his Jewish friends in Plonsk. Szlama found it surprisingly easy to mingle with the goyim, especially since he'd never been as rigidly orthodox as his father. To him, the goyim seemed like normal people. Szlama always attended weekly Shabbat services with his father and brothers, but he also enjoyed eating juicy hunks of roasted pork kielbasa that he bought from the market stalls on the sly.

TWO

Fewer than twenty-eight kilometers from Plonsk and forty-two kilometers from Warsaw was the town of Zakroczym. Although close in proximity to Plonsk, Zakroczym's Jews had none of the Plonskers' fragile peace with their goyim neighbors.

In 1897, Zakroczym had the highest percentage of Jews in its history: 2,211 out of 4,218 people were Jewish. In 1898, the Zionist movement became active for the first time. The interwar period, however, saw a decline in the Jewish population and their importance in the town.[1]

Equidistant between Zakroczym and the town of Nowy Dwór Mazowiecki stood the imposing Modlin Fortress, which dated back to 1806 when Napoleon ordered the bridgeheads on the Vistula River strengthened. Spanning 2,250 meters, it was then and remains today the longest building in Europe and the second longest in the world.[2]

In August 1920, during the Polish-Soviet War, all Jews from Zakroczym and the other towns near the Modlin Fortress were temporarily displaced to allow room for the Polish army during the Bolshevik offensive. During the Jews' absence, their property was partially plundered. According to the 1921 census, there were 1,865 Jews in Zakroczym. The Zionists were still influential, but the dominant party among Jews was the Agudah, whose politics did not include Zionism.[3]

In the 1930s, anti-Semitic activity increased in Zakroczym, especially through boycotts of Jewish trade and workshops. In November 1934, there were anti-Jewish riots that continued for some days. Thugs attacked Jews and looted their property. Similar activities took place in 1936. Gangs of anti-Semitic youths threw stones at the synagogue and at nearby Jewish houses, smashing their windowpanes.[4]

Josef Friedman eked out an extremely modest living as a peddler in Zakroczym by purchasing vegetables from local farmers and selling them in Warsaw for a small profit. There was very little else he could do to make money. To avoid conscription into the Polish army during World War I, he had chopped off three of his toes after his mother threatened to commit suicide if he joined. He limped for the rest of his life.

Baila Friedman, a rabbi's daughter, was a strict, religious woman who kept a kosher home, even before her father moved in with the family. Despite their economic hardship, though, the Friedman family was never hungry. Chaja helped with the chores, including milking the family's cow. When she was ten, the cow kicked her in the forehead with its rear right hoof, and she received a one-inch scar that never faded.

My mother, Chaja, was the third of four daughters born to Josef and Baila Friedman. The oldest was Rachma, born in 1917. Lieba followed in 1920, then Chaja on March 14, 1923. Eight years later in 1931, Peyru, an adorable blonde baby, completed the family.

Chaja loved cooking and baking beside her mother. Together they prepared typical Eastern European Jewish staples such as *yagda*

bilkes (blueberry scones); honey, sponge, and apple cakes; challahs; cheesecakes made with Baila's homemade cheese; pickles; borscht; *lokshen kugel* (noodle pudding); cholent (bean, beef, and potato stew); stuffed cabbage; and cabbage soup.

There was a large vegetable garden in the yard, and by Chaja's account, the Friedmans were a close, happy family. She remembers their home as having a dining room, a parlor, three bedrooms, a kitchen, and a basement, as well as a separate horse shed. There was even a sukkah (temporary hut) during the weeklong harvest festival of Sukkot, which would be in keeping with Baila's orthodox upbringing.

To provide enough wine for all the kiddushes (blessings for wine) and for the Pesach (Passover) holiday, there was a fifty-liter urn in the basement where the wine was stored. Lieba would frequently go downstairs and sneak a sip. One year, she drank so much that when Passover came, Josef scratched his head, wondering where the wine had gone.

The Friedmans never had any excess, but they had what they needed, and at times, a little more. For example, a luxury Josef couldn't live without was music, and occasionally he'd hire musicians to play klezmer (popular Eastern European Jewish music) for the family. There was also enough food to share with Jewish soldiers from the Modlin garrison, whom Baila frequently invited for Shabbat.

Chaja's parents also spent some of their money to make life easier for a redheaded neighbor boy. Red hair was very unpopular, and this boy was afflicted with a particularly fiery hue, making him a huge outcast. To help him garner friends, the Friedmans bought him a record player in the hopes that it would increase his popularity.

Such was the generosity and goodness of this family: a mother who stretched her meals to feed multiples, and a father who valued music and charity above material goods, even though they did not have excess money. For example, when Chaja was six and she desperately wanted an umbrella, the latest fad at the time, her parents wouldn't come through with such an unnecessary luxury, no matter how much she cried.

Chaja was an exceptionally good student who planned on receiving a high school education at Gymnasium when she completed her studies at the school in Zakroczym. In keeping the laws of Shabbat, which began on sundown every Friday, Chaja attended school only Monday through Friday, skipping Saturday classes. It was not a coincidence that her teacher chose Saturdays to tell the rest of the class exactly what to expect on upcoming exams.

Despite missing these reviews, Chaja still scored the highest grades and was periodically beaten up by the goyim boys because of it. Chaja was such a good student that Lieba purposely stayed behind a few years in school so she could receive help from her sister. By 1939, Rachma, the oldest sister, was waitressing at an upscale restaurant in Warsaw to help raise the money needed to send Chaja to Gymnasium. But she would never attend.

THREE

Once again, life's crueler rhythms collided with the Baijgel family, this time upon Yosef's early death in 1927 when Szlama was about fifteen. The second Mrs. Baijgel remained in the home, just as Josef had hoped, and continued to care for his large family. Still, the family structure changed.

Szlama gave up the poultry trade and apprenticed with a tailor, believing it to be a more stable trade. The oldest brother, Cheel, was now a barber. Itchele, the third youngest, became a kurnik. However, he was a playboy who loved good food and beer, and his earnings disappeared in the taverns, where he invited his friends to share roast duck and tall glasses of Baltic porter.

Gradually, the Baijgel boys grew up and left home. Szlama fell in love with a young woman named Tovah Goldin, and they married in 1934. He had steady work in his small tailor shop, and the couple soon welcomed a daughter.

The only darkness on the horizon was the news from Germany, which was now reaching Plonsk with alarming frequency. In 1932, the Nazis became the majority party in the national parliament, the Reichstag. Adolf Hitler became chancellor of Germany in 1933. In 1934, the elderly German president Paul von Hindenburg died, and Hitler used emergency powers granted to him by the Reichstag to abolish the office of the presidency. He then banned all political parties but his own National Socialist (Nazi) Party, dismantled the democratic Weimar Republic, and established the Third Reich, installing himself as the dictator, *der* Führer, the sole leader of the German nation and all Germanic peoples.

In rapid order, Hitler broke all of Germany's obligations under the post–World War I Treaty of Versailles, thus absolving the billions of marks Germany still owed in annual reparations payments. He also reoccupied the Saarland, the Ruhr, and the Rhineland, which the Allied powers had seized in 1919. In response to foreign disapproval, Hitler blamed his actions on a conspiracy of Jewish bankers and leftist politicians.[1]

Still, this was happening in Germany, not in Poland, many Jews reassured themselves. With Josef Piłsudski's death in 1935, however, the anti-Jewish sentiment he had been able to hold at bay began to rise to the surface. The "protection" offered by Polish authorities was very uneven after his death.[2] The stability he offered evaporated, and a crisis began.[3]

With all state power consolidated in his hands, Hitler launched Germany on a path that few could have foreseen in the 1920s. He reintroduced military conscription, further defying Versailles's restrictions on rebuilding Germany's army, navy, and air force. Because these services were essentially new, they were equipped with the latest tanks, artillery submarines, and aircraft. Massive spending on the rearmament program helped raise the German economy out of the Great Depression.

After years of propaganda meant to gain the German population's political support, the Nazis finally unveiled their true policies on September 15, 1935, with the passing of the Nuremburg Laws. These were a web of harsh and complex anti-Semitic regulations.

It was now illegal for Jews and gentiles to marry or have sexual relations. Jews were stripped of their property and expelled from their professions. Anti-Semitism had always lain at the heart of the Nazi doctrine. Their core beliefs included two founding myths: that Germany had *not* been defeated on the battlefields of World

War I but rather had been "stabbed in the back" by Jewish bankers and capitalists; and that Jews had secretly banded together with Communists to undercut Germany.

Jumping on the bandwagon, Polish anti-Semitic political parties put increasing pressure on the new post-Piłsudski government to pass legislation that would place restrictions on the social mobility of Polish Jews. The first example of this legislation was a bill enacted into law on January 1, 1937, placing limits on the practice of the kosher slaughtering of cattle by Orthodox Jews. This bill allowed the Polish government to regulate the number of cattle allotted to kosher slaughterers. Furthermore, jurisdictions in which Jews numbered less than 3 percent of the total population were permitted to outlaw kosher slaughtering altogether. This blatantly discriminatory bill struck directly at the heart of the religious practice of Poland's large number of Orthodox Jews. It also had a devastating effect on the economic well-being of tens of thousands of Jewish butchers, their families, and their suppliers.[4]

The Polish parliament never passed the anti-Jewish laws, but Jews were excluded from the civil service and armed forces. Jewish businessmen were increasingly hard-pressed to obtain state loans. Jewish workers were unable to procure employment in Polish-run factories. Jewish students were denied access to universities, and teachers were barred from jobs in state-run high schools. Religious shopkeepers were forced to keep their stores closed on Sundays, a large post-Sabbath Jewish shopping day.[5]

In March 1938, the Polish government announced a new Citizenship Law. This law stated that as of October 30, 1938, the passports of Polish citizens who had lived abroad for more than five years would be revoked if those citizens had not "maintained contact with the [home] country."[6] Although this law did not target Jews specifically, its effect had a dramatic impact on Jews who lived outside of Poland. One such community was the tens of thousands of Polish expatriate Jews residing in neighboring Germany. The Polish action effectively rendered these people stateless on German soil, making them a German problem.

Nazi officials, particularly SS (for Schutzstaffel, the Nazi security, surveillance, and terror agency) chief Heinrich Himmler and his subordinate, Reinhard Heydrich, had planned since earlier in the year to force Jews, particularly Polish Jews, to leave Germany. Between October 28 and 29, the SS and Gestapo (for Geheime Staatspolizei, Nazi secret police) detained fifteen thousand Polish Jews, stripped them of their valuables and possessions, and sent them over the German frontier into Poland.[7]

For Szlama, these rumblings were upsetting, but they didn't have much impact. He and his family had been exposed to anti-Semitism, so these types of laws were not exactly new and seemed to come and go depending on who was in power. He was focused on his young family and continued working at the tailor shop.

FOUR

It is so easy for us in the twenty-first century to question why so many Jews, including the Baijgel and Friedman families, remained in Europe during Hitler's rise. Some did leave. In Germany alone, over half of the Jewish population (approximately 304,000) emigrated during the first six years of the Nazi dictatorship.[1]

Poland was home to some 3,300,000 Jews, many who were living in or just above the poverty line.[2] These people simply didn't have the means to leave. And Jews who could afford to go elsewhere found picking up their lives and moving to a foreign continent too daunting. Imagine leaving your home, your extended family, your livelihood, your language and culture, all because of some distant, albeit horrible rumblings from another country.

Most people in Poland's small towns didn't know about the racial laws in Germany. They *did* notice a mass influx of Polish Christians coming into the country from Germany after being kicked out for not being Aryans (ethnic Germans), however.

But it was far easier for people to assuage their fears with the *facts* at the time. Poland had a nonaggression pact with Germany that began in 1934, as well as military alliances with France and Great Britain.[3] Many people comforted themselves with the idea that, if the worst should happen and Hitler invaded Poland, France and Great Britain would immediately come to Poland's aid, and the unpleasantness would all be over quickly.

Even the Munich Agreement, signed a year before the war, on September 30, 1938, by Germany, France, Great Britain, and Italy, which permitted Nazi Germany's annexation of portions of Czechoslovakia along the country's borders mainly inhabited by German speakers (the "Sudetenland"), didn't spell doom for Poland. After the Munich Agreement, Hitler promised an end to territorial demands in Europe, and he stuck to his promise for a few months. Relations with Poland were relatively cordial for this brief period.[4] But could a man like Hitler be trusted to keep his word? Most people thought the answer was yes because they had nothing to the contrary.

Further, having the financial means and the motivation to leave was not enough. Chaim Weitzman, a noted Zionist leader who became the first president of Israel, made a famous remark explaining why more Jews didn't flee Europe before the war began. "The world was divided into two: places where they could not live and places where they could not go."[5] Many countries had restrictive immigration practices for Jewish refugees, which reflected a global climate laced with xenophobia and anti-Semitism.

An international conference on refugees initiated by President Franklin Roosevelt was held in July 1938 in Evian, France. It was a complete fiasco. Of the thirty-two countries invited, only the small Caribbean island of the Dominican Republic offered prospective Jewish refugees from Germany and Austria any hope of emigrating.[6]

In the smaller Polish towns like Plonsk and Zakroczym, in the circles of families like Szlama's and Chaja's, most Jews tried to reassure themselves that things would get better. In the first years of the Nazi regime, the application of anti-Semitic pressure was uneven, which sent confusing signals to Jews. In the quiet times, they were lulled into believing that the worst had already passed.

Szlama focused on his family and his tailor shop, which were basically his whole world. As a married father and local tradesman, the borders beyond Plonsk held little interest for his reality.

In mid-1930s Zakroczym, when anti-Semitism was on the rise, Jews became a little more uneasy.

One Thursday evening, Chaja heard hushed voices from the adults in the other room. She crept a little closer to hear what they were talking about.

"What are we going to do now?" her paternal aunt cried. She owned a little convenience store that sold necessities.

"Quiet," her father said. "We don't want to wake the children."

"Wake the children? The goyim gathered in front of the store, chanting, 'If you buy from Jews, you're hurting yourself.' None of my customers came in! None!"

"They're pressuring the farmers too. I can't always get produce, dairy, or bread," her husband said. "It's not good for business, but it's not good for Jews either."

"And that's not all," her aunt continued. "On Sundays, they even went so far as to try to bar Jewish merchants from traveling to Warsaw to sell their goods there." Her voice had increased to almost a wail, and her mother and father drew close, quieting her down.

The next morning, no one looked rested. Chaja understood that the adults were upset, but she didn't understand the full implications of what was happening to her aunt's store.

The region continued its slow boil. Polish authorities refused to accept the recently deported German Jews of Polish descent. The now-destitute Jews became stranded in a no-man's-land between the two countries.[7]

Herschel Grynszpan, who had been living in Paris since 1936, was the seventeen-year-old son of one of these refugee couples. He was a devout Jew who wanted to live in Palestine but was too young to emigrate. His parents arranged for him to stay with an aunt and uncle in Paris. But because Jews could not move money out of Germany legally, Herschel had to sneak into Paris, though he stayed there for years. His parents were one of the thousands of Jews arrested, stripped of their property, and put on trains headed for Poland.

For Herschel, his parents' rejection from their country of origin was the last straw. On the morning of November 7, 1938, Grynszpan borrowed money from his uncle, went to the German embassy in Paris, and asked to speak with an embassy official. Nazi diplomat Ernst vom Rath appeared, and Grynszpan shot him five times to avenge his parents and the Jewish people for the actions taken by the Germans. He was carrying a postcard addressed to his parents that read in part, "I must protest so that the whole world hears my protest ..." Ernst vom Rath died two days later. His death was exactly the impetus the Nazis needed to unleash their hatred.

The anti-Semitic reaction in Germany and Austria surpassed all the fears of Europe's Jewish community. On November 9, 1938, in what became known as Kristallnacht, the night of broken glass, Nazi Sturmabteilung (SA) storm troopers rampaged through the streets of German and Austrian cities, burning synagogues and Jewish shops and businesses. SA thugs used sledgehammers and gasoline bombs to destroy Jewish schools, hospitals, and cultural centers. Before the night was over, almost one hundred German Jews were dead, and thousands more were dragged from their homes.[8]

The next morning, more than one thousand synagogues lay in smoking ruins. At least thirty thousand Jewish men and boys were sent off to concentration camps in Germany, such as Dachau and

Buchenwald. German police and firefighters did nothing to stop the brutality, nor did Germany's gentile population.[9]

The reaction in Europe and the United States was shocked horror. But the US still refused to raise its immigration quota. Britain, France, and the US made stern diplomatic protests, but no firmer measures against Germany were taken.[10] Some German Jews escaped to the Netherlands, Belgium, France, or Britain. A handful made their way to South America. But more than two hundred thousand were trapped in Nazi Germany.[11]

Poland's very active Yiddish press published the events of Kristallnacht extensively.[12] It was almost too terrible to consider. Kristallnacht had shown that the Nazis didn't balk at butchering their own citizens. What acts of violence would they commit if they got their hands on the Jews of Poland? Yiddish newspapers endlessly debated this. But residents of shtetels (small Jewish villages in Eastern Europe) like Zakroczym either didn't hear the news or didn't understand its implications connecting the event to their own lives.

Then, in March 1939, Hitler took the feared but predictable action of occupying the rest of Czechoslovakia beyond the Sudetenland.[13] It was becoming obvious to the people of the larger cities of Poland, like Lodz, Lvov, and Warsaw, that the threat of a Polish invasion was becoming very real.

In Plonsk, intense debates were held in synagogues and homes. People tried to reassure themselves that the British, French, and Russia's massive Red Army would come to their immediate aid if Germany invaded Poland. The growing desperation, however, gave way to absolute panic on August 23, 1939, when the newspapers reported that Germany and the Soviet Union had signed the sweeping "nonaggression" Molotov-Ribbentrop Pact, which contained a secret protocol that provided for the divvying up of Poland and the rest of Eastern Europe into Soviet and German hands, and that enabled Germany to attack Poland without fear of Soviet intervention.[14]

Poland, home to 3.3 million Jews, was now ripe for a Nazi invasion. And most of them were not going to be able to leave.

FIVE

The residents of Plonsk went to work one peaceful Friday morning in September 1939. The town began to awaken, with shopkeepers opening their stores and displaying their wares, and the bustle that accompanies workers began. Szlama had left his young wife and daughter and also began his day at the tailor shop.

A black Luftwaffe JU-87 dive bomber rolled over on its wing high above Plonsk, startling nearly everyone before it swooped down almost vertically. The plane produced a terrifying howl as it plunged toward the town. Then, at an altitude of less than one thousand meters, it released a single 700-kilogram bomb, blasting a huge crater in the old cobblestones of the market square.[1] The ground shook, and cobblestones rained down, damaging other brickwork. Windows shattered from the shock wave.

World War II had begun, although it wasn't called that until *Time* magazine coined the term ten days later, on September 11, 1939.[2]

For two tense days, Poland waited for Great Britain and France to come to her aid. Finally, on September 3, the two powers declared war on Germany.[3] Still, they were thousands of kilometers to the west, much too far to help Poland fight back Germany's tanks and Luftwaffe (German Air Force) bombers. Also, Britain and France were still traumatized by the horrible casualties and drain of their resources from the Great War (which would now be known as World War I). Their defenses were no match for the Nazis. As German forces streamed into Poland, they crushed local army formations with their new Blitzkrieg (lightning war) tactics.

Szlama and Tovah waited in terror for reliable news.

"What are you thinking about?" Tovah asked quietly.

Szlama paused. He didn't really know how to reply, whether Tovah had heard the rumors: German troops were burning villages and their inhabitants to ashes with powerful flamethrowers; the Nazis had tanks that could swim through rivers and lakes and speed through wheat fields at over eighty kilometers per hour while firing powerful cannons; Nazis were committing mass rape and slaughtering Jews. Each day, the rumors grew more terrible. "Whether we should stay or go," he said.

"How will we go?" she asked.

He thought about how he could sneak them over the border using his network of trading partners in the farms. But he didn't know how far the Nazis were or if there could be safe passage if they surrounded the border. It was agonizing. "I don't know," he replied. And so they waited.

The Germans reached Plonsk near sunset on September 5, immediately blocking the roads leading out of the city. They arrived in waves, with columns of infantrymen clothed in gray-green uniforms and steel helmets marching behind armored tanks. Next came the greatly feared SS, with uniforms bearing double lightning bolt insignias on the collars and whose officers wore metal army helmets embellished with icy silver death-heads. Every SS officer carried a whip.

A van carrying a loudspeaker rolled through Plonsk's streets ordering everyone to stay indoors until further notice. Curfew breakers, the harsh voice said in Polish, would face immediate execution.

The Germans plundered many Jewish-owned stores and began to abuse and humiliate the city's Jewish population. On September

19, all Jewish men aged sixteen and over were ordered to report to the prison courtyard at 9:00 a.m. to register their names.[4] Szlama joined over 3,600 Jewish boys and men. The registration process was accompanied by brutal beatings filmed by German photographers. Szlama couldn't help but notice, despite his fear and disgust, how professional and clean the Nazis were, how well organized and experienced they seemed.

Gestapo men came from the nearby town of Płock and took seventeen Jews and some forty gentiles hostage, among them the mayor, the regional doctor, teachers, and priests. All but one were shot.[5] The following quotes were recorded by members of the town:

> Almost all the men presented themselves at the appointed time, not possibly knowing what awaited them. Mother even encouraged Father and I not to be late ... when we crossed the prison courtyard I saw the Gestapo men standing around, roaring at the tops of their voices and kicking people with their boots ... at the end of the registration we were ordered once more to stand in a line along the length of the square and the Germans came around and pointed at those they chose ... in the end seventeen men were taken hostage at the prison. They put them into two cells: nine in one and eight in the other.[6]

> All the manifestations of a sound public life were quickly strangled by the Germans. It was impossible to meet in the street without being suspected of subversion ... all cultural and religious activities were forbidden by order of the occupiers. The Great Synagogue was destroyed, together with the artworks and Torah scrolls within. The building was turned into an egg warehouse by the Germans.[7]

The Great Synagogue in Plonsk had been built at the end of the eighteenth century. Its ark, where the Torah was housed, had taken seven years to carve and was famous for its ornate beauty. Next to the synagogue were three *batei* midrash (Jewish study hall located in a synagogue), the oldest of which was built in the style of Spanish synagogues before the Inquisition. It had been built partially underground so that its height would not attract too much attention.

Of the synagogue, David Ben-Gurion later wrote, "The Hassidim prayed in their shteibels (Yiddish for "little house" or "little room" used for communal Jewish prayer). The rest of [the] Jews worshipped at the Great Synagogue, as well as at the three adjacent batei midrash. The Plonsk Synagogue was renowned for its wonderful and beautifully decorated Holy Ark, considered one of the most exquisite in Poland."[8]

The news that the Polish government had surrendered on September 27 reached Plonsk, and with it came the order for all citizens to cease resistance to the German occupation. By October 1939, Płonsk was annexed to the Bezirk Zichenau (Ciechanów region), its name changed to the German Plohnen. Many of Płonsk's remaining Jews fled to Warsaw and the Soviet territories.[9]

The Germans randomly recruited Jews for forced labor, and Jewish hostages were given the responsibility of ensuring that the laborers left for work in an organized fashion. They were also tasked with assuring the appearance of those Jews who were registered for "gymnastics" twice a week. During one of the forced gymnastics days, between the end of September and the beginning of October, two hundred Jews were marched out of the city toward the border with the Soviet Union, where some of them were ultimately murdered. In November, the Jewish community paid a ransom of 100,000 zloty (approximately US$20,000), and the surviving hostages were released.

Zakroczym, where approximately 78 percent of the buildings were levelled, fared far worse than Plonsk. Destruction came primarily from the air, as the town was heavily bombed due to its proximity to the Modlin Fortress. Many of the town's inhabitants, including scores of Jews, were killed or wounded. A bomb fell into the back garden of Chaja's father's first cousin, killing one of his daughters who had been playing outside. After the bombardment, most of the surviving Jews fled to Warsaw and nearby smaller towns, such as Plonsk. Zakroczym officially fell to the Nazis on September 9.[10]

The Soviet Union occupied Eastern Poland on September 17, 1939, and allowed some Polish refugees, Jews and gentiles, into Soviet-occupied territory. But in the space of a couple of weeks, the Soviet Union agreed to turn back refugees from the German-occupied section of Poland.

No other exits from Poland were possible. Lithuania and Latvia had been occupied by the Soviet Union since June 1939, Czechoslovakia was occupied by Germany, East Prussia was a German province, and Hungary and Romania were German allies.[11]

What remained of town was nearly obliterated on September 28 when, despite a cease-fire, Panzer (armored tank) Division soldiers stormed the Polish Second Infantry Division, whose soldiers were preparing to surrender. Wehrmacht (German army) soldiers murdered an estimated five hundred Polish soldiers. The surviving soldiers were beaten and abused, and approximately one hundred civilians were killed or wounded. German troops broke into houses, robbing and setting them on fire, and tossed hand grenades into basements filled with terrified civilians. This event became known as the Massacre of Zakroczym.[12]

In the fall of 1939, Jews who had been deported from Polish cities annexed to the Third Reich, as well as those from surrounding settlements arrived in Plonsk. At the same time, Plonsk's Jews were ordered to stitch the yellow Star of David to their clothing. After a while, they were ordered to add the word Jude (Jew) to the star. They were forbidden from walking in the street after six o'clock at night and ordered to repay all their municipal taxes dating back to 1930. A rumor circulated that the Nazis, in response to orders to cut down on resistance, were proactively alleviating the threat by shooting strong, able-bodied young men.[13]

Szlama fit this description, and he and Tovah discussed his options as they ate dinner.

"Many Jews have already gone to Warsaw, believing they'd be safer in the capital city," Tovah told him. Her pretty face was creased with worry. She hadn't been sleeping, Szlama knew. And neither had he.

"I think I'll be safer in the east. I can flee into the Soviet zone in Bialystok and return home later." He meant when the initial savagery of the Nazi occupation abated.

"What if you're caught? They'll kill you!" Tovah fought to regain her composure in front of their daughter, who was asking for more food. But Tovah had no easy answers: staying and going both meant his life was in danger.

"They're going to try to kill me either way. I'll be fine," he said, passing bread to his daughter and caressing her face. "I know trustworthy farmers along the escape route. They'll shelter me if necessary."

They both agreed that this was their best option.

On a typically bitter Polish winter night in late December 1939, Szlama slipped out of Plonsk, trudging through fields and narrow farm lanes, careful to avoid the paved roads where German vehicles patrolled. As daylight approached, he crouched behind stone walls and hid in isolated shepherds' summer huts. Dense pine forests and frozen bogs dominated the terrain, and he carefully made his way toward Bialystock.

Bialystok was the largest town in northeast Poland, with just over one hundred thousand people.[14] Like Plonsk, half the population was Jewish. The Germans left Bialystok on September 22, 1939, once they had defeated the last remnants of the Polish army. Then the Red

Army, per the stipulation under the Nazi-Soviet Non-Aggression Pact, entered the city as its liberators, welcomed by Jews and gentiles alike. Although many Jews were aware of Soviet hostility toward the Jewish religion and culture, the overriding emotion was relief that the Nazis were no longer in control of the city.

After the outbreak of World War II, large numbers of refugees, most of whom were Jewish, began fleeing eastward from Poland. They entered Bialystok in two waves: from the outbreak of the war until the Soviets' entry into Poland on September 17; and until the closing of the German-Soviet border in December, three months later.[15] Szlama entered Bialystok during the second wave.

During the first few months of the occupation, Soviet authorities treated the refugees in Bialystok no differently than the locals. They allowed freedom of movement within the annexed territory, and they also allowed them to stay in the public buildings the refugees had appropriated for themselves. In one case, Soviet officers even housed a group of refugees in a Catholic convent, despite the nuns' objections.

The refugees' situation began to change in the spring of February 1940 after the implementation of a new law imposing Soviet citizenship on all residents of those territories, including refugees. As a first step toward tighter Soviet control, Polish identity papers were withdrawn, and Polish citizens were issued Soviet papers in their place, under the condition that they renounce their Polish citizenship. This came at a cost: the former Polish citizens would be prohibited from residing in the main cities or within a one-hundred-kilometer radius of the international border. Even more harsh, the newly minted Soviet men would be conscripted into the Red Army.

As if the refugees needed *another* reason to return to their homes, the Russians, in trying to alleviate the massive overcrowding in Bialystok, instituted mandatory registration of the homeless and then sent many of them to Siberia. So many refugees chose to return to Poland that it is impossible to know what thinned the city's population more: the fleeing refugees or the banishment of those sent to the gulags (Soviet forced-labor camps).[16]

Szlama had no idea whether his chances of surviving the war would be greater if he stayed in the Soviet Union or returned to Plonsk. Many Jews did remain in territories annexed to the Soviet Union, where they felt some measure of safety away from the Nazis. Bialystok was teeming with Jewish refugees. All the synagogues and Jewish houses of study were filled with them.

The bitter Bialystok winter of 1939/40 increased the refugees' hardships. It was too cold to sleep in the streets and parks, and the railway station was declared out of bounds for them. Lack of shelter and rising prices caused more refugees to return to their homes. Szlama stuck it out for the time being. The city became so crowded that the Soviets changed their policy and told refugees, even those with Soviet papers, that they could repatriate back to their old country of citizenship. Further persuading their return were letters from Warsaw describing the situation there as tenable, with people still living in their own homes.[17] (The Nazis wouldn't establish the Warsaw Ghetto until October 1940.) Most refugees, including Szlama, decided to return, feeling the rumors of Nazi assassinations were not true. In December 1940, exactly one year after he had left, he was back in Plonsk, much to Tovah's joy and relief.

In the time Szlama had been away, Jews from nearby smaller towns flooded into Plonsk. A Judenrat (ghetto council) had been established on July 1, 1940, when the Germans turned the Plonsk Aid Committee into the Judenrat and gave its leaders the responsibility of recruiting Jews for forced labor. The council was also charged with making sure every Jewish man, woman, and child in Plonsk wore the yellow Star of David on his or her left chest.

At the head of the Judenrat was Yaakov Ramek, a decent, honest, former tailor from the nearby town of Mlawa. Alongside the Judenrat, a Jewish police force of six officers was formed. The Plonsk Judenrat was considered by the Germans to embrace the entire region of Plonsk. The head of the labor division was Szlama's cousin, the rabidly Communist Shlomo Fuks, who often lectured groups about joining the Red Revolution. The Judenrat managed to procure food for the Jews of Plonsk, delay the establishment of the Plonsk ghetto until May 1941, and release Jews from imprisonment.

The Plonsk Jews were forced to work cleaning the city, repairing houses and streets, working in the fields, and carrying out housekeeping duties for the Germans. Professionals were put to work in factories, workshops, and former Jewish businesses that had been confiscated by the Germans and given to non-Jewish Poles. Part of the wages they received were transferred to the Judenrat, which was also aided by revenues that some of its members received from doing business with the Germans. Some wealthy Jews even paid the Judenrat to replace them with the poor for forced-labor duty.[18]

Survivor Zelig Krojn remembered the Judenrat, writing the following:

> In accordance with the demands of the German authorities, young girls would be sent from time to time to Sierpc, to work in the goose-plucking factory. After work, they would come home. The girls to be sent to this work were chosen by the Judenrat ... they would obviously choose the wealthier girls, those whose parents had the means to pay a ransom and then the poorer girls would go in their place. One winter's day, I was standing next to the Judenrat and I saw the poor girls waiting, barefoot, to leave. I pointed out the state of their clothing to [Judenrat head] Ramek. He ordered clothes to be gathered from various people and brought to them so they could dress appropriately.[19]

In the beginning of 1941, the Judenrat set up a soup kitchen that provided hundreds of hot meals every day, mostly to the refugees. It also established a children's home for forty orphans aged four to ten, administered by a teacher named Ms. Grünberg.[20]

The Nazis began to tighten the noose of torture, deprivation, and control by imprisoning Eastern European Jews into intensely crowded urban enclosures, the Warsaw Ghetto being the largest in Nazi-occupied Europe, with more than four hundred thousand Jews crammed into 1.3 square miles.²¹ There were approximately one thousand ghettos spread all over the region.

In May 1941, the Nazis corralled Plonsk's Jews into their own ghetto, situated on either side of Varsha Gasse, the street where Szlama had grown up (the street itself was *not* included within the ghetto borders).²² Szlama and his small family officially entered the ghetto on May 16, 1941. The Nazis had selected the worst part of Plonsk for the Jews, in the south part of town where the poorest gentiles had formerly resided. They kicked them out of homes so primitive they lacked electricity, and they made the Jews move into them. The gentiles were then given the nicest former homes of the Jews.

The Jews were concentrated in an area that was eight blocks by four blocks. A family of four might live in one room, and the living quarters were so close together that typhus was rampant. Food was scarce. But for Szlama and the others, they had their families, and with that, came hope.

The doors and windows of ghetto houses that faced the street were boarded up. Some eight thousand Jews were imprisoned inside these homes, half of them refugees from other towns, including Chaja's family. Many families inhabited stables and warehouses. Some Jews built rickety booths exposed to the elements.²³

A Nazi German police officer named Heinrich Vogt was charged with overseeing the ghetto. One of his sadistic amusements was to burn his victims' beards and *payot* (Hebrew term for the side locks worn by some men and boys in the Orthodox Jewish community, based on an interpretation of the biblical injunction against shaving the "corners" of one's head).²⁴ Ghetto resident Henry Ramek (Judenrat head Yaakov Ramek's brother) recalled far worse. "The brutality assaulted us in every aspect of our lives. Vogt came into the ghetto every morning at 8 o'clock on the dot. Each day he would kill four young people. He would point and call out, 'You, you, you, and you!' and then he would shoot them down. He would kill them in cold blood on the street for everyone to see and then just walk away. I saw it with my own eyes."[25]

In July 1941, the Germans marched the Jews to the courtyard behind a synagogue and carried out a *selektion* (selection for extermination in a concentration or extermination camp). Jews without documentation were ordered to stand on one side, while the Germans formed a line opposite them. Every Jew without proper papers was then forced to pass by the line of Germans, who beat them with clubs. That day, 1,200 Jews living in the ghetto without the necessary documentation were deported to the Pomiechówek camp, thirty-seven kilometers southwest of Plonsk.[26]

Rather than watch his family die of starvation, Szlama and his friend Saul Eisenberg were among the Plonskers who conducted black market trade, smuggling food into the ghetto at great personal risk.

Szlama would meet Saul outside the ghetto, near the gentile markets.

"Today is Tuesday," Szlama said. "We go west, and we try to get turnips."

Saul agreed, adjusting his big jacket.

"What do you have in there?" Szlama asked, pointing at his jacket pocket.

Saul pulled out a fistful of gold and silver coins. Then he partially opened his jacket, revealing tools hanging from loops sewn in on the side.

Szlama whistled. It wouldn't be a bad haul today. From his days as a kurnik, Szlama was trusted by scores of gentile farmers with whom he could trade on behalf of himself and others. Furs, tools, and gold and silver coins were traded for flour, eggs, smoked meats, and vegetables.

The next week, Szlama allowed his brother Freum to join them. They met in the usual place and began walking out toward the farms through narrow lanes and fields to avoid the main roads.

"Who is this farmer?" Freum asked.

"Someone I know. He has cheese," Szlama replied.

"Best not to ask too many questions," Saul said.

They walked for about thirty minutes, watching as the city faded into countryside.

Freum took a deep breath. "It's so nice to be—ouch!"

Szlama and Saul turned around. Freum had stepped in a hole, and he was holding his ankle. It was already swelling. Saul cursed softly.

Szlama walked over to his brother and examined his ankle. "It doesn't look too bad," he said. "But you'll have to stay here and wait for us to come back."

When they returned, they found Freum waiting as agreed, leaning against a tree with his leg propped up. When he saw his brother and Saul, he stood up, wincing.

He hobbled for a few steps.

Szlama shook his head.

"Please," Freum said. Sneaking out of the ghetto was one thing, but he had to be back in before nightfall. Nazi patrols would kill him if he was out at night. Such was the resolve of the SS to punish those who snuck out of the ghetto that they erected a row of low gallows strung with permanent nooses. The scaffolds were less than three meters high, so when the SS executioners kicked away the stools on which the victims stood, they were strangled only centimeters from the ground. The ghetto's inhabitants, including children, were marched out to witness these savage displays. It was a warning to all Jews: "This is how we punish those who defy the Third Reich."

"We don't have time for this," Szlama said.

"Here." Saul handed his sack of turnips to Szlama and reached for Freum, picking him up and carrying him over his shoulder like a sack of flour.

He carried him like that for four miles, never once complaining. The men reached their meeting point in the city and split up to reenter the ghetto, as agreed. They got into the ghetto undetected. If they had been caught, they would have been hanged publicly in the middle of the ghetto.

The Judenrat was aware of Szlama's activities, but they looked the other way. His missions to the surrounding countryside were helping many people in addition to his own family, and he was extremely brave in making them.

During this time of increasingly severe Nazi brutality, word reached Szlama and his brothers that Srull Moshe, the youngest Baijgel brother, was dead. Srull Moshe had made his way to Warsaw before the Plonsk ghetto had been imposed. Relatives in the capital reported that an SS patrol had stopped him on the crowded lanes of the Warsaw ghetto, searched him, and claimed they had found a hidden knife. Yet everyone who knew Srull Moshe was convinced he never would have risked arrest by carrying a weapon. More likely, the SS were looking for a Jew to kill, and he tragically intersected with them. They beat him to the ground and shot him in the back of the head. It was a horrible blow for the Baijgels.

The news unnerved Szlama, but it did not deter him from slipping in and out of the ghetto. The flour, potatoes, and turnips he obtained supplemented the starvation rations the Germans allotted to the Judenrat for distribution—rations that were being stretched even further as refugee Jews from surrounding villages were forced into the ghetto, often provoking resentment from the locals. Many of the newcomers had to find shelter in flimsy shanties thrown together from boards because no apartments remained.

Ghetto conditions were appalling and declining steadily. Infants and the elderly were starving to death, and typhus was spreading among the inhabitants. An often-fatal disease transmitted to humans by lice when they simultaneously bit and defecated on their victims, typhus was caused by the bacteria called *rickettsia prowazekii*. Infected patients suffered from delirium, rashes, abdominal discomfort, joint pain, and fevers lasting for two weeks that could soar to 106 degrees.

Thanks to Szlama, they at least had fresh food and water. They passed the long days by picking lice off one another, hoping for better days.

SIX

Chaja Friedman and her family were one of the newly arrived families to the Plonsk ghetto in the fall of 1941. As they were packing for the move from Zakroczym, the Nazis confiscated Josef Friedman's horses and cart, leaving the family with nothing of value. Other Jewish families in the town were sent to the nearby ghetto in Nowy Dwor due to the overcrowding in Plonsk. That brought the end of the existence of the Jewish community in Zakroczym.[1]

The Friedmans took up residence in a four-room shtetl house with three other families. Each family was crammed into one small, freezing room. Chaja didn't find the arrangement so bad because her family was still together. But with people living in such cramped conditions and having no way to bathe adequately, there was no way to keep typhus at bay.

As if the family's circumstances weren't dismal enough, Josef tripped and broke his already crippled right leg. Despite their circumstances, Baila Friedman, pious as always, insisted on maintaining a strictly kosher kitchen, but it was virtually impossible. Much of the food smuggled in from nearby farms, especially the meat, was *treif*. Josef was not zealously religious. He would never watch his children starve over matters of faith. "Forget kosher for once," he told Baila. "The children have to eat, so let them have a little meat and some cheese." Meat and cheese were a rarity. Mainly, the Friedmans subsisted on bread and weak tea.

To help her family, Chaja got a job scrubbing floors and washing laundry at the ghetto hospital where typhus was raging. The work left her hands so chafed that her fingers bled. She despised the job. The stench of blood and feces made her vomit, and she hated listening to screaming patients. She also claimed that the native Plonskers who ran the institution treated the newly arrived refugees such as herself like dirt. During her walks to and from the hospital, she witnessed Nazis ripping the beards from the faces of religious Jews and burning the hair while the victims were made to watch. She flinched and reflexively ran her hands over her own smooth cheeks, almost feeling their anguish.

In June 1941, the Germans surrounded Plonsk with columns of tanks and trucks towing long-barreled artillery pieces. The Wehrmacht encampments around the city became so dense that Szlama stopped sneaking out of the ghetto. More daring smugglers, who had seen the columns of military vehicles, feared that the ghetto would be bombarded, killing everyone inside.

Early on the morning of June 22, 1941, the ghetto residents learned the true reason for the concentration of German tanks and troops. Adolf Hitler had ordered his huge army to invade the Soviet Union, which was in direct violation of their nonaggression pact. The Nazis betrayed their former allies and unleashed a Blitzkrieg along a two-thousand-kilometer front stretching from the Baltic Sea to the open steppes of the Ukraine.

Barbarossa, the operation's code name, was the largest single military campaign in history. Almost four million German troops flowed into Soviet territory under the protective shield of the Luftwaffe. The resistance offered by the unprepared and disorganized Red Army quickly collapsed under the surprise attack. Within days, the Nazis struck deep toward Leningrad, Moscow, and Kiev.[2] To Poland's Jews, this was grave news. Neither Szlama nor Chaja would have any possibility of escape. The Red Army would not destroy the Nazis. Their last hope of salvation was crushed.

SEVEN

CHAPTER

The fierce Russian winter stalled the Luftwaffe at the gates of Moscow. Instead, they surrounded Leningrad and starved out the city's three million inhabitants. On the Ukrainian front, where many citizens were virulently anti-Semitic, the Germans had been largely greeted as liberators of Stalin's repression.[1] Many Ukrainians also gleefully participated in the ruthless Einsatzgruppen (Nazi mobile killing squads) slaughters, such as the massacre at Kiev's Babi Yar ravine where almost thirty-four thousand Jewish men, women, and children were shot in two days, September 29–30, 1941.[2] Victims of the Einsatzgruppen also included those perceived to be political enemies, the Roma (Gypsies), as well as residents of institutions for the mentally and physically disabled.[3]

The Nazis determined that these mass shootings proved to be an inefficient and demoralizing method of dispensing with the Jews. Even the most hardened SS members became disgusted with firing their machine guns into the naked, huddled victims forced to kneel at the side of the long burial pit they had been made to dig for themselves. After months of these mass exterminations, Einsatzgruppen troops complained of mental anguish and battle fatigue from shooting their victims, especially women and children, at such close range.[4]

The SS needed a more expedient, less messy method of getting to the Final Solution to the Jewish Question, the Nazi euphemism used for the absolute extermination of the Jews of Europe. On January 20, 1942, Reinhard Heydrich presided over the Wannsee Conference, a secret meeting in a palatial villa in the Berlin suburb of Wannsee. Here, various high-ranking Nazis responsible for security, legal, and transportation matters met to discuss their roles in the planned liquidation of the roughly eleven million Jews of Europe.

Every Jew in Western, Central, and Eastern Europe, it was decided, would be transported to six large extermination camps located in Nazi-occupied Poland. Transporting eleven million souls to six killing centers presented a monumental challenge to the already overburdened German railroad system. However, the men of the Wannsee Conference were confident they could accomplish the task.

From Poland's north to south, these camps were Treblinka, Chelmno (the first operational death camp, beginning on December 8, 1941, *before* the Wannsee Conference), Majdanek, Sobibor, Belzec, and at fifteen square miles, the largest extermination and slave labor complex, Auschwitz-Birkenau, near the border with Slovakia.[5]

The killing would be carried out using carbon monoxide from vehicle engines and with a poison gas called Zyklon-B, a powerful industrial insecticide that released deathly cyanide when exposed to oxygen. Treblinka, only eighty kilometers northeast of Warsaw, used carbon monoxide from a Soviet tank engine, as did Belzec, Majdanek, and Sobibor.[6] But this method, like mass shooting, was also unequal to the colossal task of slaughtering millions.

After experimenting on Soviet prisoners of war at Auschwitz, Zyklon-B proved to be the most effective killing agent.[7] Plans were made to expand the already enormous Auschwitz-Birkenau, using Jewish slave labor, to become the most extensive clearinghouse for murder. The operations would include multiple large underground gas chambers to induce the most rapid asphyxiation of victims, followed by coke-fired crematoria to burn the corpses. When completed, Birkenau would have a peak killing capacity of six thousand victims per day.[8] The Jewish slave laborers would die from the combination of starvation rations and grueling forced labor under punishing weather conditions. There would be a never-ending supply of fresh Jews to replace them.

The SS and the Gestapo were tasked with the difficult assignment of figuring out how to convince the Jews to board trains bound for the death camps. The men of the Wannsee Conference knew that a plausible ruse was needed to deceive the Jews. They came up with the phrase "resettlement in the east" as a vague, nonthreatening description for humanity's greatest genocide.[9]

Just nine months after the Wannsee Conference, on October 28, 1942, the first transports from Plonsk to Treblinka and Auschwitz-Birkenau commenced.[10]

Everyone in the ghetto was on the verge of panic because news of the true intent of "resettlement" had reached the city months before by way of the brother-in-law of Dr. Arthur Ber, the director of the Jewish hospital in Plonsk. Dr. Ber's brother-in-law (name unknown) had somehow managed to escape Treblinka and make his way to Plonsk. Despite his graphic descriptions, many people refused to believe his account of gas chambers and huge, smoldering pits where bodies were burnt.[11] It was just too horrible to imagine. Coincidentally, another ghetto official's relative escaped Treblinka and made it back to Plonsk.

EIGHT

The first transport of Jews to Auschwitz (also known as Auschwitz I) arrived by rail from Bytom, Poland, on February 15, 1942.[1] After arriving at the unloading ramp near the camp, they were escorted by the SS to the courtyard of the crematorium. In the meantime, all approach and transit roads to Auschwitz were cleared and closed.

After forced to undress, the entire group was led into the morgue-cum-gas chamber where they were told they were going to have a shower, followed by a hot meal and work assignments.

The moment the Zyklon B pellets were dropped into the chamber, the motor of a truck parked beside it was switched on to drown out the screams and groans of the dying. The killing and subsequent ventilation of the gas chamber lasted several hours. (Later, motorized ventilators were added, shortening the period to about an hour.)

Next, the *sonderkommando* (special workers), Jewish prisoners forced to work in the gas chambers and crematoria, burned the corpses in ovens, or outdoor pits if there were more bodies than the ovens could accommodate. The process took place in the deepest secrecy, with participation limited to the minimum number of SS men.

The Nazis found the first killing batch sloppy and inefficient. The modest capacity of the crematorium could cope with only 340 corpses in the space of twenty-four hours. This, plus the difficulty of keeping the whole action a secret, resulted in the decision to move the operation to nearby Birkenau (Auschwitz II).[2] Today, when people refer to Auschwitz, they are really referring to the highly sophisticated killing machine Birkenau grew to be. It didn't begin that way, however.

Birkenau started humbly as a farmhouse, whose original owner had been evacuated from the area. Adolf Eichmann, one of the principal architects of the Final Solution, had identified the dwelling during his first visit to Auschwitz. He ordered its windows walled up, its doors strengthened and sealed by screwing them in place, and shafts drilled into the walls. The entrance door bore the inscription *To the Baths*, and on the inside of the exit door, which opened into the open countryside, the inscription *To Disinfection* was emblazoned.

This updated gas chamber known as Bunker 1 or the Red House became operational on March 20, 1942. After the victims were killed, their corpses were buried in mass graves in a nearby meadow. The prisoners who worked in the burial detail were then killed in the infirmary by a phenol injection into the heart.[3]

Incoming transports were directed to the unloading ramp of the goods station at Auschwitz, known as the Judenrampe (Jew ramp), from where they were eventually led off to Bunker 1. Starting on July 4, 1942, incoming transports were submitted to selektions, a staple at Auschwitz, separating prisoners fit enough for work from those slated for liquidation.

The men were lined up in one column along the ramp, the women and children in another. This procedure was accompanied by the weeping and cries of people who, uncertain of their fate, were afraid of being parted from loved ones. Each column was directed to approach the SS doctor in turn, a doctor who decided based on physical appearance whether they were fit enough for work or whether they were slated for death. With a movement of his hand to either the left or the right, the doctor decided their fate. The young, strong, and healthy would be sent to the camp to work, while the rest—the sick, the cripples, the elderly, mothers with children, pregnant women, and those who seemed to have a weak constitution—were sentenced to die.

With the help of stepladders, the doomed were loaded into waiting lorries and told they were being driven into the camp. If there was not enough room in the lorries for everyone, the remainder marched behind. The escorting SS tried not to be provocative. On the contrary, they calmly dispelled fears with false information about the fate that awaited them. People must have been reassured by the outward appearance of the secluded cottage, especially in spring when the trees of the surrounding orchard were in bloom.[4]

Upon arrival to the gas chamber, the doomed were told of the baths and disinfection that awaited them and ordered to undress in the two huts reserved for the purpose. Then they were led into the farmhouse. Individuals suspecting a trick, who might spread panic in the rest, were discreetly led behind the building and shot in the back of the head with a quiet, low-caliber weapon.

Sonderkommando members helped prep the Jews who were about to be gassed, directing them to hang their clothes neatly. They cut the women's hair (sometimes doing this after the gassing). After the victims were dead, other sonderkommandos removed the corpses from the gas chamber, extracted gold teeth and fillings, and transferred the bodies for burning. Some sonderkommandos cleaned the gas chamber, while others dealt with the victims' personal possessions, sorting them and readying them for shipment to Germany. After a few months of such gruesome work, sonderkommandos were themselves executed and replaced with new prisoners.[5]

The gas chamber had the capacity for eight hundred. If the need arose, considerably more were crammed in, and if there was still overflow, they were shot immediately.[6] After the chamber doors were shut, bolted, and screwed shut, specially trained SS disinfection experts introduced the Zyklon B in the form of small lumps of diatomite (a soft, sedimentary rock) soaked in prussic acid.

Death inside the chamber occurred after a few minutes from internal suffocation caused by the prussic acid stopping the exchange of oxygen between the blood and tissues. People standing near the shafts from which the pellets were released died almost instantly, as did those who shouted, due to their more rapid respiration. The old, the sick, and children also died more quickly. To ensure that no one remained alive, the gas chamber was not opened until thirty minutes had elapsed. However, in periods when the pressure of incoming transports was particularly intense, the gassing time was shortened to ten minutes.

When the sonderkommando heard no more screaming, the chamber was ventilated to extract the gas. When it was safe to open the doors, most of the corpses were found near the door, where those inside had desperately tried to escape from the spreading gas. Bodies covered the entire floor of the gas chamber, cloven together in a traffic jam of bent arms and legs. The bodies were smeared with excrement, vomit, and blood. When the need arose, guards overcrowded the chambers with so many victims that they died standing up.

The sonderkommando removed the corpses, loaded them onto iron wagons, and transported the bodies by a narrow-gauge railway for several hundred meters to deep pits for burial.[7]

On December 14, 1943, a new sorting complex was opened to process the victims' belongings. There had initially been five warehouses, but the Nazis pillaged so many goods and valuables from the hundreds of thousands of Birkenau's victims that the initial five warehouses swelled to thirty by the end of the war.[8]

More than 1,500 mostly female prisoners sorted through the looted property in shifts. The prisoners had to search everything for valuables, because they could be hidden anywhere, including inside food containers or sewn into the seams of clothing. Anything of value had to be dropped into a locked wooden box located in the middle of the room.

The sorting complex was referred to as Kanada, a nickname given by the prisoners due to their perception of Canada's wealth and abundance of natural resources. Kanada *kommando* was one of the choicest jobs a prisoner could have. Females working in Kanada were permitted to keep their hair long and received extra food, staving off malnourishment. The prisoners working in Kanada kommando lived in barracks inside the warehouse, away from the rest of the lice-infested prisoners of the camp. When the guards weren't looking, they could steal extra food on which to survive or a pair of shoes or heavy clothing to protect themselves from the severe winter weather. Some smuggled valuables to bribe the guards or the *kapos* (inmates tasked with supervising fellow prisoners—some were Jews, more often gentiles with criminal pasts). If they were caught stealing, however, they were killed.

Because the Kanada women were generally well fed, clean, healthy, and better dressed than other inmates, the SS guards sometimes forced themselves on them, even though sexual relations of any sort with Jews was considered "race defilement."[9]

Once the belongings were examined, sorted, cleaned, and disinfected, they were shipped off to the Reich for distribution among the German people and Volksdeutsche (ethnic Germans who had settled in the General-Government, the German zone of occupation outside the borders of Germany).[10]

Due to rising amounts of Jewish transports to Auschwitz, a second farmhouse was converted and designated Bunker 2 or the White House. Next to it, three barracks were built to serve as undressing rooms for the condemned.

Bunker 2 contained four compartments with the capacity to gas 1,200 people at a time. This new chamber was used in July 1942 to demonstrate the gassing procedure in its entirety to Heinrich Himmler, the man Hitler charged with administering the Final Solution.[11]

Two months later, Himmler observed the corpse disposal method used in Chelmo that he most preferred: pyres with as many as two thousand bodies burning in layers alternating with kindling. Consequently, Birkenau adopted this approach in the disposal of its victims. Himmler also ordered the exhumation of the mass burial pits so that the remains could be burned in pyres.[12]

Seven months prior to Bunker 2's inauguration, SS Sergeant Ulmer of the Central Construction Administration of Auschwitz completed plans for the construction of Crematoria II and III in Birkenau.[13] Built by Jewish slave labor, they were fully operational by March 1942, and the systematic gassing of the Jews of Western, Southern, and Eastern Europe began in earnest. One major upgrade in the new death factories was that the undressing rooms and gas chambers were moved underground.[14]

Plans for two more gas chambers and crematoria (IV and V) were completed on January 11, 1943, this time with the undressing halls, gas chambers, and crematoria on the same level, which would streamline the process to an even higher efficiency.[15]

NINE

On October 28, 1942, the first transport from Plonsk, containing almost two thousand sick and elderly Jews, departed in sealed cattle cars on a bright, sunny morning. Dr. Arthur Ber, a physician from Plonsk who was trained in France, remembered, "The Jews were gathered in the square and ordered to hand over all their valuables, such as silver, foreign currency and jewelry, except for wedding bands. The first person in the line was stripped practically naked ... the people broke the heels of their shoes, removed their hidden valuables and dropped them into the bags."[1]

Three more transports left Plonsk in November and December. Anyone caught trying to escape deportation was publicly hanged.

At the end of November 1942, Chaja Friedman, along with her parents and her sisters Lieba and Peyru, waited in a huge crowd. Barking dogs, screaming children, and yelling soldiers moved every which way, adding to the chaos. Trucks rumbled through the mud and stopped close to the crowd.

Where were they going? And why? No one would answer her questions. Once on the truck, she leaned close to her mother and closed her eyes. Each time the truck hit a bump, she was pressed farther back. The woman in front of her pressed into Chaja, her hair going up Chaja's nose if she breathed too deeply. Only by tilting her head slightly could she manage to breathe. She couldn't wipe the sweat from her forehead. Her hands were pinned down because there were so many people pressing against her. At last the stifling crowd began to ease, and Chaja had the slightest breath of air when the truck rumbled to a stop.

"Get moving!" a solider shouted. He hit whoever was near him, whoever didn't move fast enough. The thwack of his club seemed so loud to Chaja. "Get moving! Onto the car!" he shouted, hitting an old man who was moving slowly.

Chaja could see the cattle car had not been cleaned. There were people already on the car, and she turned to find her sister, only to be pushed rudely from behind. She put her foot on the step and reached up for the handle. How many hands had been here before her? Thousands? And she pulled herself up into the stifling, dark, crowded cattle car.

They traveled for seventy-two hours without food or water, with only two pails serving as toilet facilities. Before long, the pails were filled, their contents sloshing over the sides and onto the floor. Passengers were packed so tightly they were literally on top of one another. If someone died, the corpse became a sofa for the living. Many elderly people died from the lack of fresh air. On November 28, 1942, Chaja's train came to a halt. She had arrived at Auschwitz.

There was mass confusion and chaos when the train pulled up to the Judenrampe. SS men shouted, "Alle raus!" (All out!) Snarling German shepherds were a menace to the Friedmans and their fellow passengers who'd been cooped up for days in darkness, unable to move their limbs, weak from hunger and thirst. Now they were being ordered to disembark as quickly as possible with shouts of "Raus, Juden!" (Out, Jews!) Passengers able to muster up the strength ran out of the cars. Those who couldn't cooperate as expeditiously as the Nazis demanded were beaten with clubs. The dogs growled, bearing their sharp teeth.

Quickly, the SS separated the men in one column, five across, and women and children into another. Next, mothers with small children were further separated from the rest of the women. Despite the separate columns, Chaja's family somehow managed to remain intact. Peyru's long blond braids stood out brightly among the people on the ramp. As the selektion process continued, Chaja grew anxious for another reason. In the crowded, squalid conditions of the cattle car, she had been unable to move her bowels for three days; now she was painfully constipated. It would become a chronic condition throughout her life, no doubt caused by the severe emotional trauma.

Suddenly, a tall SS man pushed into the ranks and pointed to the left side of the railroad tracks, ordering Chaja's parents and youngest sister to go in that direction.

Peyru wailed, "I am never going to see my sisters again."

She was right. Virtually every child was marked for immediate extermination unless the camp doctor selected him or her for experimentation purposes. Mothers with children too young for labor were killed to prevent the mass hysteria separating them would have caused.

A businesslike SS man approached Chaja, her sister, Lieba, and their cousin, Surah. "Can you work?" he asked, his neatly pressed uniform and neatly groomed beard a stark contrast to the rumpled, dirty appearance of everyone around her. "Yes!" they answered.

They were pushed to the right with the other young, strong people. Once the selektion process was complete, the old, the weak, and the mothers with children were loaded onto open trucks. Someone asked an SS guard where their families were going. "Those people can't walk, so we are letting them ride," he told her.

Fit for labor, Chaja, Lieba, and Surah marched into Birkenau that day along with 166 other women.

Recalling that day many years later, Surah said that they didn't know anything about Birkenau. The cousins truly believed they would be reunited with their families inside the camp. When they entered the barracks, they asked the women they found there where their families were. No one wanted to answer them.

The sleeping accommodations were primitive—rough wooden planks, three tiers high, some strewn with dirty straw. The newest inmates scrambled for a place on the boards. They were given nothing to eat or drink.

The next day, they awoke after a fitful night's sleep to a horrible stench. The air was thick with the smoke and ashes of their loved ones burning in the roaring pyres Himmler so favored.

But the older inmates didn't want to admit the truth, telling them instead, "It's the bakery." It wasn't long before the rookie prisoners learned the truth.

The worst degradation of the day occurred when the women entered the bathhouse and were ordered to undress in front of the watching SS, who were laughing and making lewd comments. Once naked, they were led into another room and told to spread their arms and legs. Male inmates employed as "barbers" added to the humiliation. Blunt instruments, dull from having shaved tens of thousands of preceding prisoners, cut and ripped their skin as every hair on their heads and bodies, even their most private areas, was roughly removed. To their further shame, naked men were brought into the same room for shaving. Many of the women, including Chaja, had never been naked in front of a stranger before, much less a male. Lieba and Chaja recognized some of the men from their town, adding to the indignity. By the end, male or female, everyone was covered in blood.

Prisoners had their heads shaved for three reasons. First, to remove their identity; men had to wear caps, while women wore headscarves, making them all look the same. Second, typhus-carrying lice thrived in human hair. And finally, having a bald head made it harder for escapees, particularly women, to disguise themselves.[2]

After a trickling shower of cold water, prisoners were sprayed with a powder disinfectant and given clothing that had belonged to previous victims. Skinny people were given clothes that were too large, and heavy people got things that were too small. It was the same with the shoes. One was lucky to get a garment that could offer some warmth, but that was a rarity because the best pieces that came into Auschwitz were shipped to the Reich.

Next came tattooing, administered by a female prisoner. Chaja became 26069. Surah, 26068, cried from the pain of the needle and was rewarded with a hard slap from a female guard. Lieba's number is not known, but it was most likely either 26067 or 26070.

After being tattooed, the women were led back to the barracks for their first *appel* (roll call). Appels were a miserable, twice-daily torment in Nazi concentration camps. All prisoners were made to line up in rows of five across to be counted, first at four o'clock in the morning and again in the evening. Even the dead had to be present for appel. Every *body*, in the most literal sense, had to be present for an accurate appel count. The roll calls were held every day, regardless of the foulest weather. The official purpose of appel was to count the prisoners, but the exercise was also another opportunity to inspect, humiliate, and intimidate the inmates. Gas chamber selektions were also routinely made during appel. Harsh reprisals, such as beatings and death, were dealt for anyone who was late or did not stand perfectly still. Prisoners had to stand at rigid attention, clad only in their thin uniforms, while the block kapo counted thousands of prisoners. If a mistake was made, the whole process began again before the tally was given to the SS officer. Some prisoners died while standing for appel.[3]

Many women, including Chaja, rubbed snow on their faces so their cheeks would look rosy and they'd seem healthier. However, if prisoners were caught *eating* snow, they were beaten. When snow wasn't available, some women intentionally dug into their skin with their fingernails to get a bit of blood to use as rouge. Chaja later recalled selektions being held as often as every third day at morning appel.

TEN

Szlama knew he could avoid the transport by slipping away to the countryside, but he could never leave his wife and daughter again. There was nothing to do but wait for the inevitable. On December 16, 1942, Szlama, Tovah, and their young daughter were loaded onto the final transport from Plonsk. It contained young people, professionals, and those considered privileged by the Judenrat. Also on board were Judenrat chairman Yaakov Ramek, his wife and two children, as well as 340 children from the orphaned children's home in the ghetto, accompanied by their teacher, Ms. Grünberg. Later, she would recall what it was like:

> At 4 am, we all stood in the square ... with our packages in our arms ... we were placed in rows, and between 5–6 am we left in a long line towards the train station. The non-Jews watching us bowed their heads and crossed themselves. (Other departing Plonskers had memories of gentiles who lined the streets clapping, as if in delight at a holiday parade. Perhaps they behaved differently this time because it was the final transport.)

> Immediately, the Germans began screaming, and
> then there was pushing accompanied by whips. We
> were barbarically forced into an ordinary passenger
> train. We used our elbows to get in faster, faster,
> without thinking of anyone else, so we could avoid
> the blows.[1]

The Germans employed both cattle cars and passenger cars for deportations—whatever was available. They did not provide the deportees with food or water, even when the passengers had to wait days on railroad spurs for other trains to pass. Those who were deported in sealed freight cars suffered more from the intense heat of summer and freezing temperatures of winter, as well as the stench of urine, excrement, and vomit, than those who rode in passenger trains. But whether in a train or cattle car, aside from a bucket, there were no provisions for sanitary requirements. Without food or water, many deportees died before reaching the camps. Armed guards shot anyone trying to escape.[2]

A small comfort for the Baijgels was that their transport did indeed take place on a passenger train, but it was just as impossibly crowded, with people sitting in the aisles. Nevertheless, it was a real train with windows, unheated but unexposed to the elements. One woman even brought her knitting and worked on a sweater. In another car, a woman gave birth.[3]

The transport arrived at Birkenau at 3:00 a.m. on December 17, 1942. When the train pulled up to the ramp, it was dark and silent. The stillness was immediately shattered by blinding spotlights and bedlam: screaming, shouting, barking, snarling.

Szlama heard a woman say it reminded her of a big city.

More trains pulled up, and the guards shouted, "Raus! Raus! Get out! Get out!" It was a mad replica of the night Chaja had arrived.

Szlama was roughly separated from Tovah and his daughter when the two were shoved to the group of other mothers and children. Szlama instinctually knew that no good could come to Tovah's group. Open trucks soon appeared, and SS guards used their whips to coerce the women, as well as the elderly, onto them. When the trucks were filled to overcapacity, they headed along the left of the farthest set of rails. As Szlama would find out the next day, Tovah and their daughter, as well as the members of the Judenrat, the children from the orphanage, and their teacher, Ms. Grünberg, were all were gassed an hour later with about 1,200 others from their transport. At the end of the war, there would only be a few dozen survivors from Plonsk.[4]*

When Szlama reached the front of the selektion line, he was determined to stand tall and look strong. Even at that early point, he knew the only way to survive was to have the will to. He lied about his birth date, shaving five years from his age, and was motioned to pass through the gate into the camp. *I will work*, he thought. *I will survive*. He knew being positive was the only way to survive.

Before Szlama entered the barracks, he was made to stand outside in the frigid cold with 346 others until evening.[5] When they were finally let in, the men scrambled like cockroaches in a newly lit room to find spots for themselves on the top rows of the primitive, three-tiered, wooden bunks, where there might be a little more air. It didn't take long to learn another benefit to being on the top: there were no dead bodies above dripping body fluids onto those below.

The barracks were severely overcrowded, with as many as eight men per bunk. If one man turned over, seven others had to turn with

---

* Albert Salomon, a Plonsk electrician in the final transport, passed the selektion and was given a job in his trade. From time to time, they sent him to the gas chambers to repair the electrical wire that spanned the walls. "At the entrance to the crematorium was a corridor that led to the undressing area … that room had a door above which was written Bathing Room … the room was full of showerheads so that the initial impression would be that it was indeed a bathing room. They pushed masses of people into there to save space. After the room was completely packed, it was hermetically sealed. They funneled the gas in via three small openings in the ceiling. Each time, I was called to fix the wires, which were torn by the people fighting their bitter deaths. These were electrical wires that were stretched across the walls, and the wretched people would tear at them in the throes of death." Zemach, *Memorial Book of Plonsk and Vicinity*, 467.

him. The only benefit to being packed so tightly was the warmth the other bodies radiated. The only way to get a blanket was to grab one from someone who had just died. But the blankets were crawling with lice, so there were two miserable options: the cold or the itching.

At 4:00 a.m., the kapos roused the men and chased them outside for their first appel. Snow had fallen during the night, and the temperature was below freezing. The sky was deep black in contrast to the glaring lights fanning out from the guard towers. The inmates were arranged five across. Szlama sought a place in the center, using the men to form a human shield from the stinging wind. His clothes did little to insulate him from the winter temperatures of southern Poland. Still, he learned a valuable lesson: always try to find a place in the middle. Aside from less exposure to the penetrating wind, the SS and kapos would be less likely to notice him. Appel that first morning was relatively short, lasting only ninety minutes.

Next came registration and delousing. The SS initiated the newcomers by marching them past the corpses, arranged like cords of wood in readiness for the pyre. Severely malnourished prisoners worked silently, lifting the stiff human lumber onto wheelbarrows. If Birkenau's newest prisoners had mustered any hopes of surviving, this macabre demonstration surely extinguished them.

Next, the men were stripped, shaved, and given a weak, cold shower. They received striped uniforms that offered no relief from the elements, and a pair of shoes from a large pile. There was no regard to size. One could have size 11 feet and receive a size 7 pair of shoes, or even a pair in two different sizes. It was common to receive two left shoes or two right ones.

Next came tattooing. Three men sat at wooden tables ready for the task. One man recorded the prisoners' numbers, one man held down the prisoners, and one man did the tattooing using a construction drill to carve the ink into the inmates' forearms. From Szlama's transport, 523 men received the numbers 83912 through 84434. Szlama became 83935. (Women from the transport, 257 of them, were given the numbers 27562 through 27306.)[6]

ELEVEN

CHAPTER

On June 23, 1942, an SS Oberführer (senior colonel) named Viktor Brack wrote in a letter to Heinrich Himmler:

> Among tens of millions of Jews in Europe, there are, I figure, at least two to three millions of men and women who are fit enough to work. Considering the extraordinary difficulties the labour problem presents us with, I hold the view that those two to three millions should be specially selected and preserved. This can, however, only be done if at the same time, they are rendered incapable to propagate. About a year ago I reported to you that agents of mine had completed the experiments necessary for this purpose. I would like to recall these facts once more. Sterilization, as normally performed on persons with hereditary diseases, is here out of the question, because it takes too long and is too expensive. Castration by X-ray however is not only relatively cheap, but can also be performed on many thousands in the shortest time ...[1]

Brack's letter was in response to Himmler's order to contact Nazi physicians who had been engaged in a program of systematically killing mentally and physically disabled patients living in institutions in Germany and German-annexed territories. After receiving Brack's letter, Himmler ordered the procedure to be tested on prisoners in Birkenau. He was looking for a way to carry out the biological destruction of all conquered nations, whose populations were referred to as *life unworthy of life*, by depriving them of their lives or their reproductive capabilities.[2]

Five months later, on November 2, 1942, a Nazi doctor by the name of Horst Schumann, who had previously overseen the carbon monoxide gassing of his victims, followed Himmler's orders and set to work on testing Brack's theories at Birkenau. He had no previous experience in this field. While another doctor, Claus Clauberg, utilized injections to sterilize women, Schumann attempted to do so by administering radiation to their genitals. He also became the doctor responsible for experimenting on male inmates. Sometimes he had the help of Polish (gentile) inmate Dr. Wladislaw Dering, though Schumann performed many of the procedures personally.

Schumann also liked to choose his own test subjects. He favored young, healthy, attractive Jewish men.[3] A survivor named Moshe Dach, an acquaintance of Szlama's from his transport, stated in video testimony that a lot of people from his transport were castrated, "the healthy-looking ones." Unfortunately, Szlama was one such test subject. Dach didn't say exactly when Schumann's victims were chosen, but by referring to men from his transport, it can easily be inferred that they were chosen immediately upon arrival to Birkenau.[4] If it had been any later, Szlama wouldn't have been *healthy* or *good-looking*.

My father never spoke of his ordeal. I learned of it shortly before his death in 1991 from the doctor who treated him during his final illness. My mother confirmed that my father did indeed have a testicle removed in Birkenau. Only a small portion of Schumann's victims survived, and some of those who did later testified about what they had endured. One male victim told of the sequence of events from the X-rays:

> "My genital organ, together with the scrotum, on a machine ... the noise of a motor ... from five to eight minutes," after which he "had a general ill feeling"; to the collection of the sperm; "Dr. Dering came with a sort of club and put it into my rectum ... Some drops came out of my member,)"; to beginning arrangements for the operation. "I said, 'Why are you operating on me? I am ... not sick.' [And Dering] answered, '... If I take not the testicle off you they will take it off me,'"; to the painful spinal anesthetic and the operation itself. "After some minutes, I saw Dr. Dering when he had my testicle in his hand and showed it to Dr. Schumann, who was present."[5]

After the war, Dering quoted in court that when asked by another victim why he was being operated on, Dering replied, "Stop barking like a dog. You will die anyway."[6]

There were gentile victims too. A group of young, healthy Polish men were subjected to the same experiment. They were given an unusually high dosage of radiation because an orderly reported, "Their genitals started slowly rotting away," and the men "often crawled on the floor in their pain. Ointments were tried, but the men did not improve. After a long period of suffering, they were ordered to the gas chamber."[7]

A prisoner doctor named Stanislaw Klodzinski, a former member of the Polish Underground, wrote that as many as two hundred men were subjected to x-ray castration. About 180 of the group had at least one testicle amputated. On December 16, 1942, ninety castrations took place.[8]

Szlama arrived in Birkenau just one day later. Due to the Nazis' meticulous record-keeping practices, we know that Szlama was given a spinal anesthetic and castrated on August 19, 1943, a full eight months after arriving in the camp. He would have been neither healthy nor good-looking by this time. However, as previously stated, it is highly likely that he was irradiated soon after arriving in Birkenau and castrated later to learn if the effects of the radiation had caused sterility in his amputated testicle. Szlama had arrived at Birkenau on December 17, 1942. Records show that just two weeks later, Dr. Schumann carried out another two hundred sterilizations by radiation on young Jewish men. After several weeks and months, he planned to have them castrated.[9]

The timeline for the sterilization experiments went as follows: After receiving radiation, the victims went to work, just like other prisoners. However, if their health became poor, either from the radiation or infection, they were sent immediately to the gas chambers. For those who underwent surgery, as Szlama later did, postoperative developments including hemorrhages and septicemia (blood poisoning) resulted in rapid death for many of the subjects. If the experiment didn't kill them, a ten- to twelve-day hospital stay was given.[10] Szlama took steam baths during his stay in the *rewier* and tried as hard as he could to keep his wound clean. In a single-testicle castration, like Szlama's, the second testicle was typically removed one to two months later.

The general estimate is that approximately one thousand prisoners, male and female, underwent x-ray sterilization or castration, and about two hundred of them were subjected to surgical removal of testicles or ovaries. These statistics are the fruit of the Auschwitz policy to keep accurate surgical records of the experiments. Many experimental records were destroyed before the camp was liberated, but there wasn't time to burn them all.[11] Szlama's records survive, listing the medical procedure, the mode of anesthesia (spinal), the name of the doctor who performed the castration (illegible, but it wasn't Schumann or Dering), and even the doctor who performed the spinal. Though Schumann didn't perform Szlama's castration, he most likely selected him from the Judenrampe.

Szlama was very fortunate in two counts, the first being that the radiation dose administered to him was indisputably low. The logic behind the experiment was to be able to produce sterilization with the *least amount* of radiation, in other words, more quickly and efficiently. To that end, varying levels of radiation were administered to the test subjects. If one was administered a very high dose, he or she became too ill to return to return to work and was sent to the gas chamber.[12] Because Szlama fathered two sons after the war, he was undoubtedly exposed to a very low dose of radiation.

In a place where luck couldn't be counted upon even once, Szlama got lucky twice. Only one of his testicles was ever removed. Somehow, he slipped through the cracks, and the Nazi doctors never came back for his second testicle. In many cases, the second procedure was conducted with noticeable brutality and limited anesthesia because there was no longer any reason for the doctor to be secretive in his intentions, as with the initial castration.

For those who survived at least in the short term after the second surgery, death usually followed quickly from more advanced physical weakness, drop in morale, and the likelihood of being sent out to work immediately after the procedure. The Nazi doctors had their sterility results, and the subject was expendable.[13]

In a report to Himmler on the influence of x-rays on human gonads dated April 29, 1944, Dr. Schumann concluded that castration by radiation should not be considered as the method for mass sterilization due to its costliness. Rather, surgical castration, he was convinced, took only six to seven minutes and was, in comparison with castration by x-ray, significantly faster and more reliable. Dr. Schumann closed his report with the hope that he would be able to report on the continuation of these experiments soon.[14]

TWELVE

Newly arrived prisoners appeared every few days, a fractured mix of nationalities. Some were Germans who had arrived in civilian passenger trains, dressed as if for a proper trip. Some were Dutch, often tall and blue eyed. Others were darker Czechs and Romanians. Virtually all were Jews. Separated from the Jews but treated just as miserably were the Seventh-Day Adventists and the Gypsies, who had their own separate camp.

Of all the native European lands, by far the worst fit for the subhuman lifestyle in Birkenau were the Western Europeans, who as a group had enjoyed a more refined and less physically demanding existence. They had lived in homes with the comforts of indoor plumbing, heating, and electricity. Many had desk jobs that were not physically demanding and didn't have the daily struggles of existence, such as procuring food and water, to worry about. They were less muscular. They were soft. In contrast, most Eastern Europeans were used to hard work and getting by with little. Even more advantageous in a death camp, they were used to working hard while being hungry.

Prisoners who had been around the block in Birkenau had their own slang term, *muselmänner*, to describe those who had shrunk to such a level of emaciation and lack of affect that they were literally the walking dead. Muselmänner were resigned to their impending death and were largely unresponsive to their surroundings.[1]

Survivor and writer Primo Levi explained:

> All the muselmänner who finished in the gas chambers have the same story, or more exactly, have no story; they followed the slope down to the bottom, like streams that run down the sea. On their entry into the camp, through basic incapacity, or by misfortune, or through some banal incident, they are overcome before they can adapt themselves. Their life is short but their numbers are endless; they, the muselmänner, the drowned from the backbone of the camp, an anonymous mass, continuously renewed and always identical, of non-men who march and labour in silence, the divine spark dead within them, already too empty really to suffer. One hesitates to call them living: one hesitates to call their death, death. With the word 'muselmänn', the elders in the camp designated, for reasons unknown to me, the weak, the infirm, those who were doomed to be singled out.[2]

Some scholars argue that the term possibly comes from the muselmänner's inability to stand for any length of time due to the loss of leg muscle, thus spending much of the time in a prone position, recalling the position of the *musselmän* (German for Muslim) during prayer.[3] As a group, Western Europeans degenerated into muselmänner much more quickly than Eastern Europeans. No human, however, was equipped to last very long under the backbreaking energy expenditures and lack of caloric intake.

Chaja's first kommando assignment was digging trenches in the frozen earth. The cold metal shovel felt like fire in her hands. She knew if she slowed her pace, she'd be beaten by the guards, most likely with the butt of a rifle. She'd already seen another woman spit out bloody teeth after such a beating.

Chaja's job digging trenches soon ended. Next, she was part of a group of women tasked with salvaging bricks from homes that had been burned in the towns adjacent to the camp. After separating the bricks, she had to clean them of any mortar and soot, then carry up to ten at a time, *while running*, to the collection pile, where they were stacked in groups of two hundred, precisely arranged in opposite directions, just so. The women were beaten if so much as a piece of dust was found on a brick.

What the women couldn't know or even possibly imagine was that the bricks they were so painstakingly cleaning were being used to construct the new, more modern crematoria. Even Himmler's mighty pyres and the two small gas chambers currently in use were no match for the millions of Jews and other enemies of the Third Reich whom the Nazis were planning to exterminate.

Chaja had just finished setting her bricks into the pattern and was on her way back to the pile when a guard's voice boomed and all movement ceased.

"What is this?"

Chaja turned around. *Please, please don't even look at me,* she thought.

The guard's normally immaculate black boot was covered in dust because he had been kicking the pile Chaja just left. Now the bricks were scattered.

"You!" he said, pointing to a girl who was shrinking, trying to get away even as she dropped her bricks.

Surah!

Chaja turned and ran, the sounds of the guard hitting her cousin seeming to get louder, not softer, as she left to get more bricks so she wouldn't stand out as idle.

This was only one of the ways guards amused themselves with the women. Another way was to choose a random woman and have her lie on the ground. They would then place the middle of a shovel handle on her neck and stand on opposite sides of it, teeter-totter style, rocking back and forth until she died of a broken neck. The remaining inmates would have to carry the lifeless body back to appel.

The worksite was a few miles away from the camp, and sometimes there were as many as four dead bodies to haul back. The women fashioned stretchers out of wood scraps lying around the kommando site. It was in their best interests to get those corpses back. If even one body was missing from appel, they knew, they would be made to stand all night until it was time for work in the morning.

It had already happened. The women were so scrupulous about dragging corpses back to the camp, yet someone had been unaccounted for. It was very likely that she had vanished into the mud or feces of the toilet facilities. Chaja and the rest of the woman had spent the entire night kneeling in the rain with their arms up in the air. If the guards saw an arm move even the slightest bit, they beat her with a stick.

As the days wore on, many women stopped caring if they lived or died. Some jumped into the electric fence that surrounded the camp. The current was so strong it had the capability to suck someone who was standing too close right into it. Other women simply stayed in the barracks, refusing to go to appel, courting death.

Guards also utilized appel as an opportunity to hold selektions, plucking women who'd been brutalized by their kommando guards beyond the capacity to work, as well as the weak, the sick, and the dead. The dead and the nearly dead were sent off to Block 25, along with women caught hiding in the barracks. Block 25, everyone knew, was the holding pen for the gas chambers.

Chaja realized she had to find ways to increase her daily food intake, even though the Nazis' strategy was to starve and work their labor force to death and then simply replace them with fresh inmates.

Chaja's headaches would not stop, and she felt weak and dizzy. She saw food everywhere: she dreamed of it, she thought she smelled it, she thought she tasted it. But there was no food, except for a tiny bit of ration.

She was used to seeing women talk about food. They discussed so many recipes, spices, what food looked like. Yet despite this camaraderie, the women fought, pulling hair, punching, kicking. Women who were from diverse backgrounds, even some who were educated, it didn't matter. They fought over anything, everything. Chaja learned to keep to herself and away from everyone else.

The days took on a foul rhythm. The women rose before sunlight. No drinking water was given to them for the first six months they were in Birkenau, only the bitter tea, whose contents were a mystery. Water was such a precious commodity that the Nazis put no salt into the rations since salt created thirst and they wanted to minimize the craving for water. Prisoners were even willing to trade their bread for salt.

Surah described their morning drink as a tea made from "little flowers." Some women used a portion of this precious liquid to wash their faces. They were not permitted to urinate or defecate in the morning, only at night. To get to the latrine, a slice of lumber with holes running along its length set atop a ditch, they had to walk through deep mud. There was no grass in Birkenau because they ate every blade as it sprouted in the muddy spring. The women grabbed handfuls of the fresh, sandy grass and added it to their weak tea to help fill their bellies. They called this mixture *pemosa*, which had no true meaning but helped give the earthy mix a semblance of nutrition. There wasn't much nourishment in the grass, but the stalks gave the women something to chew.

If a woman got stuck in the mud, she lay there until she died. If she was unfortunate enough to fall into the ditch of excrement and urine, she suffered the same fate. Pity from fellow inmates, even relatives, was rare. The women were too focused on their own survival. They lived like animals.

In the evening, each woman received a small piece of bread, about one-quarter the size of a piece of today's store-brought bread, along with the watery soup that held no real nourishment and a little piece of margarine. For an eighteen-hour workday, the total calorie intake was about five hundred calories. If one tried to save any of her bread, either by putting it under her head while lying down or in her armpit, it would be stolen by morning. It was better to eat it right away. To augment what little she was given to eat, Chaja grew adept at stalking women on the verge of death. She hovered near them so she could salvage their rations the moment they took their last breaths, before anyone else got the opportunity.

In the three-tiered bunks, twenty women needed to find the space to sleep. There was maybe some dirty straw but nothing on which to rest one's head. If there was a blanket, it had to be shared by as many as seven women. Everyone fought and pulled for a piece of the thin, lice-ridden fabric.

The women slept in the only clothes they had, which were wet and filthy from living and working in them day after day. To add to the misery, all the women were covered in crawling lice, despite being showered with delousing chemicals and given a change of clothes every six weeks. The bugs jumped from their bodies onto their bread. Chaja ate the lice, feeling them crack in her mouth. Picking them off was simply too laborious.

The day after delousing, when they were as clean as they were likely to be, the women had their blood drawn for transfusion into wounded German soldiers. This practice was ridiculously out of sync with Nazi ideology, whose propaganda brainwashed thousands of people to believe that Jews were subhuman vermin. In fact, it was a crime to engage in sexual intercourse with a Jew, yet Hitler mandated that Jewish blood was good enough for the war effort. It was just another example of illogical Nazi doctrine.

THIRTEEN

CHAPTER

By Szlama's second morning in Birkenau, he began to measure his life in days, silently chanting, "I will survive today." This became his mantra. It was too generous. More seasoned prisoners were counting their lives by the 1,440 minutes of every day. Death was always imminent. As if the hundreds of Jews arriving daily, slated for death, weren't enough, the SS also had a daily quota of killing to fulfill amongst the labor force. Workers were beaten to death or shot at their kommandos for nonexistent infractions. But, like in the women's camp, many of these unfortunates were culled from appel. As Szlama was standing in line that second morning, he was randomly pulled out of his row by an SS officer and punched in the face. He crumpled to the ground. Sensing that the officer would be back to collect him, he ran to another row farther back and elbowed his way in. When the officer approached him again, Szlama endured another punch, but this time he was ready. He had planted his feet firmly on the ground and received the blow without moving a muscle, possibly passing some sort of test. The officer moved on.

Szlama instinctually knew to volunteer for any job that was asked of the men. If he could continue finding ways to be useful, he might have a better chance of surviving, whether he had any actual skill or not. When a kapo asked if any of the men had ever mixed mortar before, Szlama stepped forward. How hard could it be? Luckily, it didn't require a master craftsman to mix sand, cement powder, and water. But there was still room for failure. If he didn't get the recipe just right, he'd have too brittle a mix or one too soft. He must have gotten it right, because he survived the week he spent on this kommando.

By the end of his first week, Szlama recognized that his biggest enemy other than Nazi barbarity was hunger and death from natural causes. The Nazis had a never-ending supply of fresh laborers rolling into the camp every day. The rudimentary gas chambers in place at Birkenau were grossly inadequate for the numbers of Jews pouring onto the Judenrampes every day. The masonry work being performed by Szlama, Chaja, and hundreds of other prisoners, building the more modern and efficient crematoria, was to be Birkenau's salvation in helping the Final Solution come to fruition. The sooner the inmates starved to death, the sooner they were replaced with stronger, fresh prisoners. The typical life span of an inmate performing heavy labor was measured in weeks. Szlama was expending too much energy and receiving barely any calories. The only thing he had going for him was his history: he was used to working hard, and he'd lived with privation. But after the war, he always maintained that hunger was the worst pain he'd ever endured.

Szlama was switched to the carpentry kommando. He climbed ladders with stacks of masonry-framing lumber on his shoulders. It was depleting the little bit of energy he had, but he still refused to give up, even as he watched the inevitable descent of the men around him. Somehow, he persisted.

Next came roadbuilding. This was by far the deadliest labor assignment. Many starving prisoners, still grasping their picks and shovels, fell gasping to the frozen ground. Like pouncing dogs, the kapos used their clubs to rouse them to their feet, but many had simply given up. The SS guards grabbed the men by their shirts and dragged them to the side to await the wagon that would take them to the gas chambers.

As Szlama watched the numbers of his original work crew dwindle, he resolved to do all he could, short of stealing food from fellow prisoners, to stay alive. When grass began to sprout at the roadsides of his worksite, the men, like the women, grabbed it by the handful and gulped it down. It was more a psychological boon than a nutritional one. Szalma was starving to death now, growing weaker every day as his body began to consume muscle tissue. Any fat he'd carried on his frame was long gone. He was sliding into muselmänn status, but he still clung to his survival mantra. *Another day.*

FOURTEEN

Sometime in the spring of 1943 while on a visit to the latrine, Szlama was surprised to meet Freuim, his second youngest brother. Although Freuim was still in his early twenties, Szlama was shocked by his appearance. He looked like a stooped old man. His skin was stretched taut over his bony skull, and his eyes were huge and vacant in their sockets. Of course, Freuim was probably thinking the same thing about Szlama's appearance. But there was one stark difference between the two brothers. Freuim was wasting into a musselmänner. His feet were in particularly bad shape. Without good shoes, one was as good as dead in Birkenau.

"Please, please give me your shoes," Freuim begged.

But Szlama didn't give the plea more than a fleeting thought, even though he loved his brother. "No," he said.

Freuim implored, "Szlama, you're clever. You can get another pair."

"No." If he gave Freuim his shoes and couldn't secure another pair for himself, he would die. It was agonizing, but there was never any question of his giving away his shoes. The months in Birkenau had deadened him emotionally. He was keeping his shoes.

Nevertheless, he despaired that he was now truly alone in the world. Freuim had been the last living member of his family, and he died in the camp. Later in his life, reflecting on the tragic decision he'd been forced to make, Szlama agonized over being faced with such a request and having to turn his brother down. It was easy to recriminate himself later, with a home, a family, and a full belly. But at the time, there was never any doubt about what his choice had to be.

FIFTEEN

Szlama had lied about having prewar experience in every job he volunteered for in the belief that it would help prolong his life. Had he not been so clever, strong, and resourceful, his inexperience could have hastened his death. But he performed all the tasks asked of him capably enough and avoided raising the suspicions of the guards.

During an appel in early autumn of 1943, the SS asked for a kurnik to fatten the geese for the SS's upcoming Christmas feast. Finally, a job where Szlama legitimately had previous experience! He volunteered immediately. This may be the loophole that spared him from his second castration.

Throughout the entire period that Auschwitz was in existence, a total of some 8,000 to 8,200 SS men and some two hundred female guards served.[1] If one-fifth of that number worked in the camp per year, more than 1,600 guards were employed during Christmas. Even if only higher-level SS members feasted on roast goose for their holiday dinner, it still amounted to a lot of work for the kurnik. Since he was providing a valuable service, Szlama knew his life was worth something to the guards. But when the geese were slaughtered, he could be too.

Sitting in the pen with the geese, away from harsh physical labor and without the scrutiny of the guards' watchful eyes, Szlama saved his energy and was left in peace. He was as lucky as one could be in a place such as Birkenau. He truly began to believe for the first time, *I think I'm going to live.*

Aside from the guarantee of living three more months until Christmas, there was one other huge benefit to being a kurnik at Auschwitz. He could use the goose feed to fatten himself.

Szlama requested three times more feed than was necessary: a half kilo of cooked noodles per day per bird. The surplus could be bartered for clothing, canned food, vodka, and gold, the latter useful in trading for more food and other goods he needed. One survivor put it this way: "The dead body had a piece of bread. I'm taking this piece of bread from this dead body and I'm taking this one pair of boots and I can sell it. With this I can buy myself a place to live. I can buy myself a place to sleep. With this bread, I bought myself a bit of access [to wash]."[2]

Equally important, for the first time since being in Birkenau, Szlama would have enough water to drink, even warm water for washing, because he also received metal pails and an unlimited supply of water for cooking the noodles. After a year in the camp, bathing was a luxury beyond imagining.

The goose pen was close to SS headquarters, but the guards left him alone. Every morning, he was marched from his barracks to the pen. In a shed adjacent to the pen were dry noodles and a barrel of water. He had the makings for starting a fire, and his first task of the day was boiling the water for cooking the noodles. Once they were soft, he carefully inserted a tin funnel into each goose's beak and poured a ladleful of noodles down the gullet of each bird.

Szlama regained a lot of strength, filling out his frame during the three months he worked as a kurnik. He feasted on warm noodles and water and barely burned any calories during this time. As he'd predicted, he was able to smuggle noodles into the barracks and trade them for all the valuables he'd imagined he could: gold coins, sardine cans, bread, and warmer clothing. He consumed traded perishables immediately so they couldn't be stolen while he slept. The canned goods and gold he wisely and surreptitiously buried in various hiding places throughout the camp for use at a future time. Looking back after the war, he occasionally thought of the hidden valuables he hadn't had the opportunity to dig up. He knew other prisoners had engaged in the same practice. It would have been intriguing to return to the camp in search of the riches he knew were buried there.

During this time of bounty, Szlama received an unorthodox delicacy. One night, as he was standing outside the barracks, a cat wandered by. Other than dogs, lice, flies, and humans, he had never seen a living thing in the camp. Perhaps it was a pet belonging to a camp official. Szlama's movements became automatic; his instincts were no different than a hungry animal's. He swooped upon the cat and snapped its neck. In the barracks, he showed its lifeless body to some of the other men. Word quickly spread through the building. Before long, someone produced a makeshift blade. The building had a brick stove on each end that was only occasionally lit, and tonight was one of those nights. The men briefly discussed whether to eat the meat raw or take the time to cook it. Szlama balked at eating a raw cat. Since he'd been the one to find it, his decision prevailed. Szlama and the knife's owner took the cat back outside for butchering. The blade was dull; it took some time to cut the cat's pelt and eviscerate it. Szlama felt his stomach contract at the mere thought of eating meat again. Finally, the job was done. The men roasted the cat whole over the stove. It seemed to take forever for the flesh to go from raw to rare. The smell was intoxicating. When it came time to eat, the men tore at the meat without bothering to taste it. It was more urgent to chew, swallow, and attempt to fill their hollow, long-empty spaces.

The SS were apparently satisfied with their nice, fat Christmas geese, because instead of killing Szlama at the end of his tenure as a kurnik, he was transported out of Birkenau.

SIXTEEN

CHAPTER

Chaja was among the lowest class of prisoners in Birkenau, fated to hold the worst jobs among the women. Even though she was clever and had been heading for a higher education, she had no discernable skills. She wasn't a seamstress or a musician. She couldn't sing or speak multiple languages, and her looks were average. In other words, she was of no special use to the Reich or to the camp. Yet even in the misery of Birkenau, there were other prisoners outside of the Kanada kommando for whom life wasn't so wretched. One would think that the bulk of the prisoners suffered equally, but there was a hierarchy in Birkenau. Those at the very top were called elite prisoners. One such woman was Mala Zimetbaum, and most everyone, including Chaja, knew Mala. To this day, her story remains one of the most powerful legends of Auschwitz.

Mala was a Polish Jew who had moved to Belgium as a child. She arrived at Birkenau only two and a half months before Chaja. But unlike Chaja, Mala was fluent in Flemish, French, German, English, and Polish. She was also highly attractive. The SS chose her to serve as a courier and a translator, thus giving her relative freedom to move about the camp. She quickly earned her captors' trust. Mala could have used her privileged position to see to her own needs and focus on surviving until the end of the war. No one would have faulted her.

To survive in a concentration camp, it was a requirement. Even so, Mala chose to help prisoners, and in this way, she resisted the terrible inevitability of being dehumanized by life in Auschwitz.

Survivor Anna Palarczyk, a close friend of Mala's, explained in her memoirs, "Resistance in Birkenau was to help each other survive. And Mala was eager to help; that was deeply rooted in her ethics."

One of Mala's responsibilities was to assign patients newly released from the *rewier* (hospital) to work details. "It did not matter whether they were Jews or Poles or whatever. Whenever possible, she sent the weaker ones to a place where the guards were not that strict or work was not that heavy, so that these people had at least a small chance to survive," Anna Palarczyk recalled.

Mala also warned patients of coming hospital selektions, urging them to ask for discharge as quickly as possible. She saved many lives, including a woman who recounted in memoirs displayed at the Holocaust Museum, "My sister-in-law and I caught typhus, so we decided to report sick. Somebody told Mala we were about to be transferred into the camp hospital, and in front of the SS guards she shouted at us: 'You lazy bitches; you are absolutely fit. Go to work! Forward!' When we came back from work in the evening, we learned why Mala had done everything to keep us from entering the ward. That day, all the people in the camp hospital had been gassed."[1]

Mala also made full use of her position to carry out assignments for the camp resistance, even managing to replace the identity cards of women selected to be gassed with those of women who had already died.[2]

"Mala's character was exceptional," remembered Tzipora Silberstein, another survivor who knew her. "This young woman did hundreds and thousands of good things for all of us. There were transports from Greece and she would stand near the Germans, writing things down. Many times, I heard that she only pretended to write, thus saving many people's lives."[3]

With her relative freedom of movement, she had the capability of encountering male prisoners. She met a Polish political prisoner named Edek Galinski, who had arrived on June 14, 1940. Mala and

Edek fell in love. Edek planned to escape with his friend, Wieslaw Kielar, but their plans changed when Kielar lost a pair of SS uniform pants he needed as a disguise. Edek chose Mala to join him instead, telling Kielar he would somehow send his own stolen SS uniform back to him so he could have another chance to escape.

The plan was as follows: Edek would dress up as an SS guard, and Mala would be dressed up as a prisoner whom he was escorting to a worksite. She'd be wearing a pair of overalls over a dress that could pass for a men's shirt when tucked inside the overalls. She would carry a large porcelain washbasin in such a way that it hid her hair so that the guards would not be able to identify her as female. Mala wanted to escape so she could tell the world what was happening in Auschwitz. Some accounts claim she carried smuggled documents hidden under her clothes.

Edek would use a forged pass, and the guard would open the gate. When they got far enough away, Mala would dump the washbasin and remove the overalls to reveal a pretty dress. The couple would pretend to be an SS guard and his girlfriend out for a stroll.

Edek succeeded in bribing an SS guard to supply him with a uniform, while Mala filched a pass from the guard room. On June 24, 1944, Edek marched out of the camp with Mala.[4]

In the book *Beyond Judgment*, Primo Levi wrote the following:

> They left in disguise and got as far as the Slovak border, where they were stopped by the customs agents, who suspected they were dealing with two deserters and handed them over to the police. They were immediately recognized and taken back to Birkenau. Edek was hanged right away but refused to wait for his sentence to be read in obedience to the strict local ritual. He slipped his head into the noose and let himself drop from the stool.

Mala had also resolved to die her own death. While she was waiting in a cell to be interrogated, a companion approached her and asked her, "How are things, Mala?" She answered: "Things are always fine with me." She had managed to conceal a razor blade on her body. At the foot of the gallows, she cut the artery in one of her wrists. The SS who acted as executioner tried to snatch the blade from her, and Mala, under the eyes of all the women in the camp, slapped his face with her bloodied hand. Enraged, other guards immediately came running: a prisoner, a Jew, a woman, had dared defy them! They trampled her to death; she expired, fortunately for her, before being put on the cart taking her to the crematorium.[5]

Chaja had already seen too much horror to be affected by the many stories just like this that were the norm in the camp. Everything seemed to exist to support the evil that was the Nazi guards, and survival required expending as little energy as possible on anything ... even emotion.

SEVENTEEN

CHAPTER

Chaja felt like an old woman. Sometimes her kommando walked by the Judenrampe. She tried to avoid watching the grim selektion process of the new arrivals, but one day she couldn't help witnessing the grisliest display of cruelty she'd ever seen. A tall, sturdy woman in her twenties had been pushed into the line of mothers with young children. She cradled a baby of perhaps eight months in her arms. Just as her group was condemned to the gas chambers, an SS officer came forward and stopped her. He looked her over and pinched her cheek and arm to assess the amount of flesh and muscle on her body. Apparently satisfied that she could survive several months of productive labor, he demanded her baby. Horrified, the woman refused. The nonplussed officer reached forward to grab the baby. Before he could touch it, the woman swatted his gloved hand away and clawed his face. Enraged, the officer clubbed her to the ground, simultaneously grabbing the baby by its clothing. Then he carried the wailing baby at arm's length, as if it was a piece of stinking garbage, turned it upside down with one tiny foot in each of his fists, and ripped the baby in two pieces. Holding his gruesome trophy by its feet as blood dripped onto the snow, the guard sang a song about the blood of the Jews. The nearby dogs became excited by the smell of blood and began barking, their growls drowned out by the shrieks of the baby's mother. Then guard threw the flesh on the ground, marched back to the hysterical mother, and continued clubbing her. The entire spectacle took less than a minute. As if nothing out of the ordinary had happened, Chaja's kommando was pushed along. This is the moment Chaja lost her faith in God.

Chaja had arrived in Birkenau just four months shy of her twentieth birthday. Now, she looked twice that age. She'd stopped menstruating, like every other nonprivileged female inmate. She was unworldly enough, however, to believe that her lack of a period was due to an additive the Nazis put in her food, rather than severe malnutrition. After all, she had menstruated in the ghetto even though she'd been hungry there.

Chaja wasn't alone in her reasoning. Many Eastern European Jews showed a general ignorance pertaining to the facts of life. But there was a psychic component interrupting the women's cycles as well—terror. Even women who were menstruating when they arrived at the camp abruptly stopped.

One study found that amenorrhea (absence of menstruation) occurred in 94.8 percent of the women during encampment, with 82.4 percent experiencing cessation of menses immediately after internment. Only 0.6 percent of women menstruated longer than four months after internment. After liberation, though, all but 8.9 percent of the women resumed menstruation within the first year.[1]

Along with menstruation vanished the shame of nakedness for many of the women, but not Chaja. She always felt humiliated, even though inmates, male and female, were fully exposed practically as often as they were dressed. They were ordered to line up naked when they were headed for the bath, the disinfection area, or a selektion. Survivor Ana Novac wrote, "Thousands of naked people next to one another—this (was) nothing human but a herd ... Any sensitivity (was) as ludicrous as it (was) futile."[2]

Survivor Zofia Posmysz described the washing facilities as such: "One liter of water in the bowl used for eating had to suffice for everyone. Inmates poured water in the hollow of their hands and washed their genitals. A guard was strolling up and down behind the wire. The sight of the figures with their legs apart did not bother him any more than his presence bothered us."[3]

Everyone, male and female, became accustomed to the sight of nudity. However, if men encountered naked women, the sight was very depressing to them. One male survivor remembered, "A few hundred women were waiting their turn to take a bath. A compressed heap of naked, hairless skeletons looked at us with dim, completely expressionless eyes, and only dry flaps of skin hanging from their chests indicated that these had once been women of life."[4]

Birkenau was meant to kill any feeling of femininity, as evidenced from the quote of another male survivor. "A procession of female (inmates) came from the women's camp. A few hundred women with shaved heads passed us ... The lack of water for washing, (lack of) underwear, and even the most primitive facilities had caused their indescribable condition. These were no longer human beings, but only some apathetic humanoid automata, masks without life and expression. When we passed their column, we got a whiff of a stench that took our breath away."[5]

In stark contrast were the omnipresent guards. Chaja couldn't help being in awe of their clean, tidy appearances, their sharply pressed uniforms, and shiny, polished boots, just as Szlama was when he had first seen them march into Plonsk.

EIGHTEEN

CHAPTER

Janina† was a large coal mine that had been erected in 1907 by Compagnie Galicienne de Mines, a French mining company located in the town of Libiaż Mały, about eleven miles west of Auschwitz. The Nazis repurposed it into a concentration camp on September 4, 1943, after I. G. Farben acquired it to supply coal to its chemical factory in Monowitz (Auschwitz III).[1]

Before September 1943, a nearby British POW camp had formerly supplied workers to the mine, but the Brits' productivity was so low that I. G. Farben executives pressed to have prisoners from Auschwitz sent there instead. Auschwitz commandant Rudolf Höss authorized three hundred prisoners to replace 150 British POWs. Among the Auschwitz group were professional bricklayers, carpenters, and metalworkers charged with expanding Janina so it could accommodate nine hundred Auschwitz prisoners by the end of 1943.[2]

The expansion was complete by December 2, 1943, and about one hundred more prisoners were transferred in from Auschwitz that day. Less than three weeks later, Janina had 509 prisoners, and by the

---

† During the war, Janinagrube changed its name to Johannagrube and then to Gute Hoggnungsgrube, but when recalling his time there, Sam always referred to the place simply as Janina.

end of February 1944, there were almost six hundred. Szlama, who was transferred there between December 1943 and January 1944, was one of these prisoners. Eighty percent of Janina's workforce was Jewish, and the other 20 percent were Polish, Russian, and German.[3]

Szlama didn't know why he was transferred from Birkenau to Janinagrube, one of more than forty Auschwitz slave labor subcamps, usually located at German industrial plants and farms.

The average life expectancy for Janina's Jewish prisoners was four to six weeks.[4] Their strength faded quickly because of the unhealthy working conditions, the lack of protective clothing and proper food, and abuse by the supervisors. Even if one avoided accidents, the most common being fractures and internal injuries, loss of life was commonplace.[5] Gentile prisoners fared better because they received more food and less brutal treatment from the guards.

Living quarters in Janina were nearly identical to those in Birkenau, except that the sleeping bunks had two tiers instead of three. There were as many as six men in each bunk, in barracks that held between 150 and 200 men. Surrounding the camp was the ubiquitous double row of electrified barbed wire.[6]

Szlama was immediately put to work extracting coal three hundred meters underground in the wet, freezing mine. He wasn't even there an hour before his clothes were soaked through. As he moved deeper into the mine to get the coal, he saw water. He wondered how deep it was; it seemed to flood part of the shaft. He noticed other men going in and went in also. It turned out to be about waist deep, and it was freezing. The mine's three shifts lasted from 6:00 a.m. to 2:00 p.m., 2:00 p.m. to 10:00 p.m., and 10:00 p.m. to 6:00 a.m.[7] He would often have to stand in that water to mine his coal, wiping water from his head also because it dripped relentlessly from above.

When he wasn't standing in water, he was lying in tunnels for hours at a time in places where he could not assume any other position. The ceiling and sides were inches from his body, and he could barely raise his arms up to pull the coal out. Sporadic dynamite blasts exploded with no warning—smashing rushes of air that seemed to suck the breath right out of his body.

Life at Janina was every bit as dreary and desolate as it had been in Birkenau. Every morning when he came out of the mine, he walked two miles back to the barracks and took a cold shower, but he had to redress in the same wet, filthy clothes. Then came a breakfast of watery soup made with potatoes, carrots, or rutabaga. Sometimes noodles or beans were added, and less often, a piece of meat. But such rations, combined with the punishing labor, brought on a quick loss of muscle mass and subsequent starvation. If Szlama could elbow himself to the end of the soup line, his portion was a little thicker because the solid bits fell to the bottom of the pot. Everyone knew this trick, so he wasn't always successful. The day's rations also consisted of about eight ounces of bread with some margarine, jam, or sausage and a cup of bitter ersatz coffee.[8]

In the mine, Szlama had a weak carbide lamp containing a flame that often blew out. Since Jews were forbidden to carry matches or lighters, he had to work in the dark until he met up with a foreman who could relight it for him. The only other illumination came from dim 25-watt lightbulbs hung sporadically in the tunnels. One prisoner, Zenek Moskowicz, found a way of lighting the lamp using electric wires from a signal bell without the use of matches, but when he was caught doing it, he was accused of sabotage and sentenced to death. Fortunately, the camp commandant commuted his sentence because he was convinced that Zenek had intended to improve the lamp. In any case, Zenek was forbidden to use his invention. Conditions in the mine were so dangerous that the guards didn't even venture into it, instead staying near the elevator shaft to make sure no one tried to escape.[9] The absence of the guards was the only advantage to working underground.

Soon Szlama was becoming a musselmänner. He couldn't survive unless he got more to eat. Fortunately, he had smuggled some his gold coins into Janina. His fellow Jewish prisoners had nothing valuable to trade for the coins, but the paid Polish employees did. Szlama was able to barter for vodka and warm clothing, which he subsequently traded for food. In this way, he kept death at bay. If he had been caught trading, he would have been executed, but it was a necessary risk. He would have died without augmenting his rations.

Early one morning, Szlama was working on a blasting crew deep in the earth. Once the blast opened a section of the cave, he and others began laying lumber and metal to build a track that would carry the coal cars farther into the mine. He pushed the car behind him back a little so he could line up the rails—when a loud metallic sound caused him to stand up.

To his horror, he could see in the dim light that two loaded coal cars had suddenly broken loose from the small electric tractor that was pulling them. Szlama was standing on the track with another coal car behind him.

Szlama panicked. Where could he go? It was too narrow to jump out of the way of the runaway cars. Within seconds, the cars smashed into him, pinning him in place and breaking his collarbone.

In the seconds after the crash, Szlama tried to move his arms. He couldn't lift his left one. He tried to grab the coal car, but his hand slipped with all the coal. He pushed the rest of the coal out of his way and got enough of a grip to extricate himself from the cars.

An injury that left his arm limp like this would render him unable to work. It was a death sentence. Once a week, like clockwork, trucks came to transport the weak, the injured, and the dead for liquidation in Birkenau.[10]

Szlama hadn't survived this long to give up now, though. There were plenty of wood slats used to build the trolley track within his reach. He picked one up with his good arm and, with the help of some men working nearby, used rags to tie it in place, keeping his wounded shoulder secure. If the bone moved the wrong way, it could puncture the left upper lobe of his lung and kill him just as surely as the guards would if they learned of his injury. But since the guards never ventured past the elevator shaft, Szlama was successful in hiding it. He continued working with one arm until the bones healed (albeit incorrectly, one on top of the other) and he regained the use of his left arm.

NINETEEN

Chaja and Lieba had been in Birkenau for about six months by the summer of 1943. Undoubtedly, having each other to live for helped sustain the sisters, but Lieba was beginning to weaken. There was no snow to rub on her cheeks, and it probably wouldn't have fooled the guards anyway. Lieba was slipping away. During her last appel, Chaja tried to physically support her by standing so close they were almost attached. The guard walked back and forth through the women, weeding out the sick. When he reached Lieba, he said nonchalantly, "You."

Chaja almost collapsed as Lieba was pulled from the line. Without Lieba, Chaja had no interest in surviving. "If you take her, take me too!" she yelled boldly. "Take me!"

She was rewarded with a slap across her face so violent she spat out broken teeth. Enraged, the guard said, "You can still work! You're strong. She's weak." He continued strolling through the rows.

It was the final blow for Chaja. Taking care of Lieba, ensuring her sister's survival, had been her only motivation to live. Without Lieba, there was no reason to keep suffering. Now she welcomed death.

In hoping to join Lieba and the rest of the Friedmans, and in utter apathy for her fate, Chaja returned to the barracks after appel and refused to leave. For six weeks, she remained inside, waiting to be dragged away to the crematorium. But for some inexplicable reason, the guards never came for her. To gain some small comfort after Lieba's death, Chaja shared her bunk with a friend from Plonsk named Nacha Ruchel, and the two women pretended *they* were sisters. At night, they would listen to the Greek girls sing songs and wonder where they got the strength to create such beautiful music.

One day, after no apparent coaxing from anyone, Chaja joined the living again, taking her place at appel and going out to work. I have a theory as to why the SS didn't kill her: it was more painful for her to remain alive.

One morning, Chaja sat next to her cousin Surah. Her thin clothing was no match for the cold, hard bench. "Are you okay?" she asked.

There was no reply.

Chaja just stared straight ahead.

"I don't want to even live anymore," Surah said quietly. "I just want a piece of bread, one day of freedom, and then to die. I don't care anymore."

Chaja just patted her hand. She didn't answer, because there was no answer. Some women didn't even want what Surah wanted. They just wanted to die.

So far, both women had survived fifteen months in the camp.

In January 1944, Moshe Dach, the Plonsker who'd been on Szlama's transport, was also transferred to Janina, initially as a bricklayer building the barracks for approximately fifty SS employed there. When the barracks were completed, Moshe went to work in the mine. For a year, he worked from dawn until dusk. He claimed that he didn't see sunlight for the entire year. Like Szlama, Moshe had an accident; in it, he tore off a large chunk of flesh from one of his hands. And like Szlama, he did not inquire after any medical care, knowing he'd be killed if he did. Instead, he cleaned the wound with his own urine and tore his dirty shirt into strips to bandage it. He couldn't move his fingers, so he sought work outside of the mine and was lucky to be given a job cleaning the room of what he called a "good Nazi."

The Nazi gave him bread and food and talked with Moshe. He told him, "You are better off than I am. I didn't volunteer for this. They took me. I have a family in Yugoslavia. We have a farm. The war's coming to an end." He purposely left the radio on and newspapers around while Moshe cleaned. "Help yourself," he told Moshe. "But if you get caught, don't tell them I left it for you." Moshe shared whatever he read in the papers with his fellow inmates.[1]

Unfortunately, the man was transferred soon after. Before he left, though, he told Moshe, "No one will ever know what happened here."

TWENTY

By early 1944, it was clear that Germany was losing the war. The Allies had achieved air superiority and were bombing German industrial cities almost daily. This forced the Luftwaffe to divert most of its fighter force to the defense of Germany, sharply reducing its production of bomber aircrafts. German air power was deeply eroded around the periphery of German-controlled Europe, where pilot losses reached exceptionally high levels.

Adding to the demise of the Germans were the Allied bombing campaigns. The large-scale destruction they caused stunted German manufacturing of war material, transport, and energy supplies and forced German industry away from the most threatened regions.[1]

Hermann Goering, the longtime chief of the Luftwaffe, made the following remarks during several interrogations in the summer of 1944:

> I knew first that the Luftwaffe was losing control of the air when the American long-range fighters were able to escort the bombers as far as Hanover. It was not long before they were getting to Berlin. We then knew we must develop the jet planes. Our plan for their early development was unsuccessful only

because of your bombing attacks. Allied attacks greatly affected our training program, too. For instance, the attacks on oil retarded the training because our new pilots couldn't get sufficient training before they were put into the air.[2]

Heavy bombing of Nazi territories forced Hitler and the German leadership to think of radical ways to combat the Allies. Huge resources were diverted to make way for production of long-range artillery weapons called Vengeance, or V weapons, to be launched from the coast of France. Their use had a limited but devastating impact. At their peak, one hundred Vengeance rockets were launched every day, their speed making them virtually impossible to intercept. V rockets caused approximately eighteen thousand mostly civilian deaths.

Nicknamed "doodlebugs" due to their engines' distinctive buzzing sound, the V rockets were a desperate attempt by the Nazis to wrest back the tide of war in their favor. But the campaign was akin to using a grain of sand to stop a tsunami. By October 1944, Allied forces in France overran the last Vengeance launch sites in range of Britain. The program had failed. Hitler, however, being loathe to surrender even if doing so meant preventing the destruction of his country, had one last-ditch effort to unleash.[3]

In June 1944, a group of Hungarian Jews arrived at Janina almost immediately after reaching Birkenau. They were still fit, except for the aftereffects of their cattle car trip. Survivor David Yeger recalled first seeing Janina's prisoners: "I saw a lot of men, but one man stood out to me. This one man was looking in the building from the outside. When he entered the building, he started begging for food, thinking from our fit appearance that we had some, when in fact we hadn't eaten in days."[4]

David was talking about Szlama, who seemed closer to death than life. His appearance shocked the newcomer.[‡]

[‡] Many years later, the two men met in New Jersey for the first time. David immediately recognized Szlama (Sam in the United States) as the face,

There were many attempts to break out of Auschwitz's subcamps, not as closely guarded as the main camps, and Janina was no exception. When a drainage ditch was dug in the summer of 1944, the camp administration discovered a subterranean passage that began near the latrine and exited under the fence. Three gentile prisoners—a German, a Russian, and a man of unknown origin— were responsible for digging the tunnel. At a later hearing, SS Camp Leader Hermann Kleeman testified, "[They] had attempted to escape by digging a tunnel underneath the wire fence. This was reported by inmates themselves because they feared the consequences." The execution of a gentile German prisoner was unusual, and Kleeman evidently remembered it more clearly than he did the executions of Jewish inmates.[5]

Later in the year, a German kapo and a young Polish Jew succeeded in escaping, with the aid of an underground tunnel. Both men got as far as Essen, almost nine hundred kilometers west, likely the German's hometown. Unfortunately, they were captured and brought back to the camp. The SS informed the lined-up inmates that this would be the fate of all who dared to flee. They hanged the escapees in the camp's roll call area.[6] David Yeger remembered being forced to watch the hanging. For lesser offenses, a typical punishment was twenty-five lashings to the naked body.[7]

On December 16, 1944, against the judgment of his top military aides, Hitler ordered an attack by his mobile reserves on a weakly defended section of the Allied line in the Ardennes region of Belgium, France, and Luxembourg. He believed an offensive could succeed if he split the Allies, forcing the Americans and British to settle for a separate peace independent of the Soviets. In doing so, Hitler callously sacrificed his own forces on the eastern front, which he knew was a lost cause.[8]

Hitler foolishly believed that success on the western front would give the Germans enough time to design and produce more advanced aircraft, U-boats, and tanks, leading to an inevitable German victory.

with its starved appearance and desperate eyes that had made such an impression on him in Janina. He'd never forgotten it.

Adding to his imprudence was his theory that Americans were not able to fight well because they were an inferior race due to the melding of so many nationalities in its citizens.

At first, poor weather conditions and overcast skies favored the Germans. The Allied Air Force was unable to fly. But it was a different story on the ground. The Allies fought bitterly to block German access to key roads. The thickly wooded forests where the Allies were entrenched were also a benefit, as the trees slowed down the German advance, giving the Allies time to add more troops. When the weather cleared on December 23, Allied fighter bombs decimated German armored divisions. Rather than breaking the Allied line, Hitler's grand scheme only created a bulge in it, thereby earning it the name Battle of the Bulge.[9]

By January 25, 1945, it was all over, and the bulge was eliminated. Hitler had sacrificed his last reserves and his greatest concentration of armor in a scheme that never had a chance of success. He dealt a severe blow to German morale on the western front, and he played into Russian hands by fatally weakening his forces in the east.[10]

The Russians marched into Warsaw on January 17, 1945, after the city had been destroyed and abandoned by the Germans.[11] That same day, Chaja withstood her final appel in Birkenau.

TWENTY-ONE

Chaja and her cousin Surah were two of 10,381 women incarcerated in Birkenau on January 18, 1945. Early that morning, Camp Commandant Richard Baer assembled a team of evacuation leaders and ordered them to liquidate all prisoners who dragged their feet or attempted to escape. The Red Army was advancing on the outlying areas of Krakow, only sixty-seven kilometers away. All the camp's human evidence needed to be purged.[1]

Before sunrise, the Nazis came into the barracks, yelling and screaming, banging on walls and grabbing people roughly by their shoulders, hair, whatever they could grab. Chaja was rushed out of the barracks with the others. They all knew the war was coming to an end because the soldiers in the camp were old; the younger ones had been transferred to the Russian front. The same was happening all around her: emaciated women braced themselves against the brutal cold and knee-deep snow. A full-blown blizzard had begun the previous evening, and it was impossible to see anything but white.

The SS were shouting, "The camp is closing; you'll be evacuated. Forward! March!"

Chaja had no idea where they were going, but she got into her column. The prisoners were formed into columns of five hundred, given some bread, and marched out of Birkenau at short intervals.

"As we formed into a ragged column," remembered survivor Sara Nomberg-Przytyk, "SS men escorted us with dogs on each side. We walked through a valley of death formed by the bodies of the prisoners." After a few hours, Surah's skin became "completely peeled from my feet. I could feel the blood swishing around inside my boots."[2]

A total of 5,345 women left that day, walking three kilometers to Auschwitz I, where they waited for the formation of the final evacuation columns from the various subcamps. The last column from Birkenau left sometime in the afternoon.[3]

The SS whipped the women to a running pace, telling them they'd be shot if they couldn't keep up. The wind was so strong and the women so light that they formed human chains to keep from blowing away. They continued to drag one another along, letting go only to release someone who had died.[4]

Ruth (Raizl) Kibel recalled after the war, "In a frost, half barefoot, or entirely barefoot, with light rags upon their emaciated and exhausted bodies, tens of thousands of human creatures drag[ged] themselves along in the snow. Only that great, strong striving for life and the light of imminent liberation, ke[pt] them on their feet."[5]

True to their promise, the SS shot anyone who couldn't keep pace, making the marchers drag the corpses to the side of the road. The SS themselves made up the phrase, "Every hundred meters an SS milestone," meaning another corpse.[6]

The Germans marched tens of thousands of prisoners out of the camp toward the town of Wodzisław, more than thirty-five miles away, where they loaded them onto open freight trains. After marching all day, the prisoners stopped at night because the SS, well fed and appropriately clothed, couldn't walk any longer. Of the tens of thousands of prisoners who went on the march, about fifteen thousand died from exhaustion or were murdered.[7]

It was impossible to keep track of how long the women marched. Survivor Herta Goldman recalled, "You couldn't stop for a minute or step out of line. Whoever stepped out of the line got a bullet in the back. If a woman sat down because she had no strength left they didn't waste a bullet on her. They hit her with the rifle butt and as they passed by on both sides of the row, they pushed her aside into the snow where she would freeze. I asked a German who passed by me, 'Tell me, where are we going?' He said, 'We have no destination. Our purpose is for all of you to drop dead on the way.'"[8]

For the Nazis, any Jew's death during the march was a benefit because, in fact, they *did* have a destination, the camps of Germany, and every survivor who reached them would add to the logistical nightmare.

How did Chaja survive such an ordeal? She never spoke of it. Surah marched out of Auschwitz wearing her striped camp uniform "with a little sweater underneath."[9] Perhaps Chaja had *organized* (common term in the camp for trading or stealing) a warm coat and a pair of sturdy shoes. Without either, especially shoes, she surely would have perished. Maybe she covertly stole such items from the corpses strewn at the side of the road. Perhaps a sympathetic German threw some bread or a potato to her, and she'd been fortunate enough to catch it without being attacked by fellow marchers driven mad with hunger. A few villagers did throw bread, but most people watching the prisoners pass were indifferent or openly hostile. The marchers, visible human wrecks, were jeered and spat at and had stones thrown at them. Most citizens refused them food and drink, and some even rounded up escapees and returned them to the SS.[10]

Accounts vary as to how long Chaja and Surah marched, but it was likely four days and nights. If there wasn't a barn around at night for the prisoners to seek shelter, they simply slept in the snow. Many died from hypothermia or were shot when they couldn't rouse themselves quickly enough in the morning.

Survivor Livia Szabo Krancberg wrote the following in her memoir:

> The guards pushed us inside [a shack] with their rifle butts. It was so dark inside ... All that time [my sister] was feeling with her feet for a place to settle down. She finally found one. However, it was

between two sleeping bodies, or we thought they were sleeping. She asked me to occupy the empty space as she settled next to the body at my right. [She] assumed the bodies were not asleep and began talking to them. She asked them to kindly move over so we sisters could be together. She promised them food. The bodies failed to respond ... At dawn, we woke up to hysterical sounds. We opened our eyes to see screaming girls pointing at heaps of corpses all over the shack. It occurred to me to look at the bodies near me. I let out an inhuman scream. "They're dead! I slept among corpses!"[11]

After sleeping among them, the women were ordered to form the corpses into a pile, one on top of the other. To add to their horror, many of the prisoners had known the dead from the camp.

We marched on country roads with neat little houses on both sides. The sun rose and the sun set and we were still marching. I saw light appearing in the windows of those homes with people, most probably keeping warm and appeasing their hunger. And we were still marching ...

At last, in the dead of the night, we stopped in front of a barn and pushed inside. Girls fell on top of sleeping cows ... The cows stood up and moved in all directions ... Some used their intuitive sense and held on to the animals' horns. Others, like city girls knowing nothing about cows, were rolling off the cows' backs and being trampled to death.[12]

Chaja's march ended almost seventy kilometers later, somewhere between January 21 and January 23, when she reached Wodzisław.

Thermometers read -20 degrees Celsius (-4 degrees Fahrenheit).[13] How Chaja survived—indeed, how *anyone* so poorly clothed, shod, and fed survived—is beyond explanation. Survivors of the death march shared the characteristics of grit and an unbreakable will to live. At the march's end, exhausted and starving, Chaja and Surah climbed into an open-topped coal car.

Survivor Edith Eisler Denes, who was only fourteen at the time, recalled, "It was snowing and it [the coal car] was open, and the snowflakes came down."[14] Besides snow falling on the women, the open coal cars had already accumulated over half a foot of snow inside. The passengers were sandwiched between snow. Unfortunately, it was polluted with coal dust and inedible.

Chaja and Surah didn't know where they were going, but they knew it would be farther west. In fact, they were bound for Ravensbrück, the second-largest all-women's camp (Birkenau's women's camp being the largest), and it was going to make Birkenau seem like a luxury hotel in comparison.

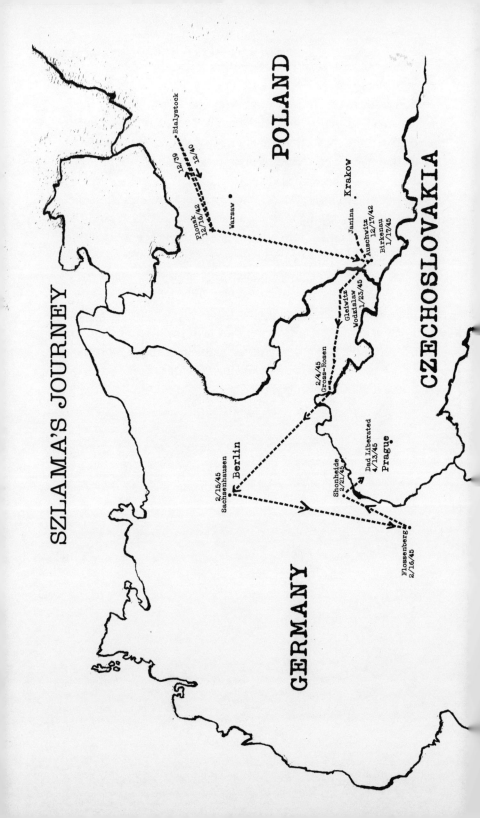

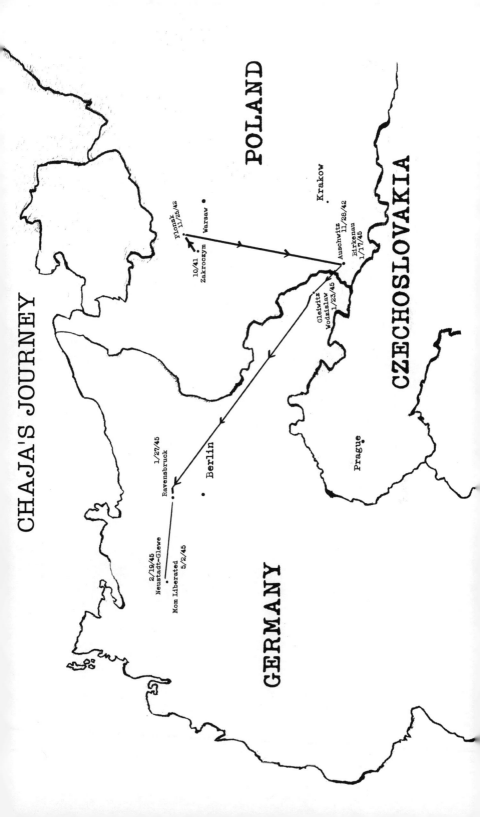

CHAJA'S JOURNEY

POLAND

Krakow

Plonsk
11/25/42
Warsaw

10/41
Zakroczym

Auschwitz
11/28/42
Birkenau
1/17/45

Gleiwitz
Wodzislaw
1/23/45

CZECHOSLOVAKIA

Prague

Berlin

Ravensbruck
1/27/45

Neustadt-Glewe
2/19/45

Mom Liberated
5/2/45

GERMANY

TWENTY-TWO

On January 17, Szlama was one of approximately 857 prisoners lined up for what was to be Janina's final appel. Approximately sixty Janina prisoners too ill to march remained behind. Sick as they were, they were the lucky ones. Janina was liberated a week later on January 25, 1945.[1]

Janina's marchers, however, were to embark on the greatest threat to their survival thus far. With no protective winter clothing, and many wearing only wooden clogs, they began what was to become an eighteen-day march, one of the longest of all the death marches from the various camps in Eastern Europe.[2] But before the actual death march commenced, they first had to trek fifteen miles to Auschwitz I, which would be the gathering point for the prisoners of all the many subcamps.

The morning of January 18, 1945, at the main camp in Auschwitz began in "great confusion throughout," recalled Filip Müller, who had been an inmate there for three years. "Early in the morning, columns of smoke could be seen rising in all parts of the camp. Quite obviously, the SS were destroying card indexes and other documents."

The prisoners were ordered to grab a blanket and some bread, if they could get a piece. Some men were given dry food, but others had nothing to eat. The prisoners were escorted out of the gate by the SS. The prisoners could hear the Russian artillery getting closer. Chaja later said they were "seized by alarm and euphoria at the same time." Would they be liberated soon, or did the SS plan to exterminate them first? The answer came quickly. Formed into enormous columns, the first of approximately sixty thousand prisoners of Auschwitz and its subcamps began the forced march west, toward Germany. "The snow crunched under our feet, a cold wind blew into our faces. We talked about nothing but where they were taking us and what they intended to do to us," said Müller.[3]

The march was a new form of torture for the prisoners. Many guards forced their columns to run without pause the entire fifty-five kilometers to the rail station at Gleiwitz.[4] Those who couldn't keep up were systematically and impassively shot.

"A few steps ahead of me," wrote survivor Marco Nahon, "I see a prisoner collapse by the roadside, completely exhausted. His face is livid. It is easy to see he cannot walk another step. An SS guard who has seen him approaches and stands before him. Very quietly, he takes his rifle from his shoulder strap, places the barrel a few inches from the poor devil's head, and shoots."[5]

Even pausing to reach down for a thirst-quenching handful of snow was a capital crime. Instead, the marchers ate the snow that accumulated on the shoulders of those running ahead of them.

Prisoners took other extreme measures to survive, such as urinating on their battered feet to keep gangrene from setting in on the wounds. If they couldn't pee, they got someone else to do it for them.

The first leg of the march stopped at Gleiwitz, where Chaja had stopped. However, while Chaja had climbed onto a coal car, Szlama and the rest of the Janina prisoners spent as much as seventy-two hours sitting in snow. The guards made fires to warm themselves, while, adjacent to them, many prisoners froze to death by morning.

Those who managed to survive the night but lacked the strength to continue marching were shot.

The next leg of Szlama's journey was among the most brutal of all the marches throughout Eastern Europe: 250 kilometers (148 miles) *on foot* to Groß-Rosen.[6] When the soles of his shoes wore through, he removed better shoes from the feet of corpses and wore those.

As always, SS guards were ordered to shoot anyone who fell behind or could not continue. They also enlisted the help of Janina's gentile German prisoners, arming them and encouraging them to take part in shooting Jews. During the Janina death march, one of these German prisoners did an "Indian dance," openly celebrating his accomplishment after killing a Jew. One survivor had the distinct impression that this guard and another were engaged in an ongoing killing competition. In another instance of cruelty, the German guards intervened to stop townspeople who attempted to give food to the Jews.

After a few days, the SS commander of the column went AWOL with the provision wagon. Some of the abandoned SS men, assisted by preferred prisoners, went to procure food from local peasants. They did not share whatever they were able to collect with the Jews. One former marcher remembers their hunger: "During the evacuation march we received no food. The Polish population in Silesia gave us, in a few localities on its own initiative, bread and milk. It occurred that the SS guards wantonly kicked over the milk jugs." Fortunately for some of the Jews, the Poles sometimes managed to slip them food, despite the Germans' efforts to prevent them from doing so.[7]

According to Janina's camp doctor, Erich Orlik, only about two hundred of the original eight hundred prisoners, in a state of extreme exhaustion, reached Groß-Rosen in the first days of February, where they were deposited into unfinished barracks for the night. For some inexplicable reason, the Janina prisoners were kept separate from the many other prisoners arriving from other camps.[8]

Possibly within hours of Szlama's arrival, Groß-Rosen and its twenty-three satellite camps were also evacuated. Szlama was ordered onto an open cattle car.[9] Although relieved of marching, the moving train made the icy temperatures and falling snow feel even more torturous, as painful as the marching had been. The men didn't have the strength to sit or stand, so they lay stiffly on top of one another for collective warmth, in a formation reminiscent of the corpse pyres of Birkenau.

Their next destination, Sachsenhausen (also known as Oranienburg), was nearly four hundred kilometers away, near Berlin. The men, still denied food, stayed in an airplane hangar. Most of them were barely alive. Because of the massive overcrowding at Sachsenhausen, they were turned out after a few hours and once more loaded onto open cattle cars, surviving on a diet of snow.

After a few hours, the train stopped in the middle of a forest. The guards opened the car doors and ordered, "All Jews out!"

Somehow, Szlama still had mental acuity to suspect the malintent of the guards.

He moved against the back corner of the car, not visible unless one was inside, and pressed himself into the corner. He was soon joined by three or four others.

The SS guard never looked inside. This late in the war, feeling they were on an aimless path, many SS were looking to escape themselves, but they still possessed enough of a membrane of allegiance not to abandon live prisoners.

The crack of hundreds of rounds of rifle fire in the distance did nothing to assure the men. Frozen, tired, starving, and absolutely mentally exhausted, all they could do was stay in hiding. Szlama was relieved when he felt the vibration of the train's engines start up again. Wherever he was going, he was still alive for now. *I will live another day.*

He was probably barely conscious when another threat presented itself. Allied airplanes strafed the train, destroying the locomotive engine. The non-Jewish prisoners and the few Jews who'd defied orders were told to get out. The snow had turned to heavy rain, soaking through Szlama's flimsy clothing, bringing a new misery. At one point, a German jeep approached the column, and the driver told the guards not to continue in the same direction because the Allied forces were approaching. The SS turned the prisoners around. As dark approached, they spotted a farmhouse with a big barn, where they spent the rest of the night. There were a few hundred prisoners left and mere hours before they would reach their destination. Most of them wouldn't live to see it.

The next morning, the guards lined the living up and continued marching them west. Szlama survived on frozen potatoes found in fields from the previous autumn's harvest. Many men suffered from diarrhea, for which they could do nothing. The mess simply ran down their legs and froze.

Szlama's death march, one of the most brutal ever recorded, concluded on February 6, 1945. He shuffled, more dead than alive, into Flossenbürg, a concentration camp along the border with western Czechoslovakia. He had survived where six hundred other men had not.

TWENTY-THREE

Designed to accommodate six thousand prisoners, Ravensbrück was the only concentration camp built specifically for women. Located about fifty miles north of Berlin, it was grossly overcrowded by 1942, with a population of 10,800 inmates. Of the 132,000 women and children who passed through its gates during the war, only 30 percent of them survived. The rest died of starvation, disease, torture, beatings, hangings, shootings, unimaginably cruel medical experiments, and, beginning in November 1944, in a newly installed gas chamber.

The most serious overcrowding at Ravensbrück occurred after the evacuation of Auschwitz when an unknown but significant number of Jewish women arrived. Death march transports from Auschwitz and other camps in the east increased Ravensbrück's population far beyond its limits to some thirty-two thousand women.[1]

Ravensbrück was infamous for the sadistic medical experiments performed there. Some women were infected with gas gangrene or bacterial infections, while others were forced to receive bone transplants and bone amputations.[2] For example, one common experiment was to amputate the leg from one woman and attempt to surgically attach it onto another. Another frequent experiment used women as guinea pigs to simulate the battlefield leg wounds suffered by German soldiers. Most of the medical subjects died or were murdered afterward, and those who survived were left crippled and disfigured. They were commonly referred to as rabbits by the Nazis *and* the inmates.[3] Other experiments involved the investigation of various sterilization techniques. Pregnant Jewish women were immediately sent to the gas chambers when they arrived at Ravensbrück, while abortions were performed on pregnant non-Jews.

Although Chaja had been relieved of marching, her ride to Ravensbrück had hardly been a respite from her suffering. She and her fellow passengers went days without eating or drinking. There wasn't even a pail on the car to use as a toilet. Survivor Hedi Solzbach remembered, "When we needed to go to the bathroom, we couldn't stand or walk, so we would have to go where we were, in our pants. It would quickly freeze and become ice, and then it would chafe."[4]

Those who could hold their bodily functions had to wait until the cars stopped to relieve themselves on the side of the train tracks under the watchful eyes of the SS.

One of the worst hardships was the knifelike pain of the icy wind hitting their skin, made more unbearable by the speed of the open-topped coal cars, "bitter, sub-zero breath," as survivor Rena Kornreich Gelissen described it. The trip took days. "I can't remember exactly how many [days] because time wasn't our main concern. Food was. Time was figured from when we last ate. Hunger and cold were our only thought. Traveling in open wagons in winter all we did was huddle against the wind and cold."[5]

Because the rail tracks had been bombed by the Allies, the cars were forced to make many stops. One particularly long delay was at a station in Berlin. One prisoner recalled, "We all fell silent as we looked around. It hardly looked like a city at all, let alone the capital of the Reich. There were mounds of rubble and just the skeletons of buildings as far as the eye could see. Over the station's loudspeaker a man's voice kept [repeating], 'Apfahren mit dem sou laden. Apfahren mit dem sou laden.' After a while I realized he meant our train. What he kept saying was, 'Away with the pig train.'"[6]

Whereas Birkenau had been run with deadly precision, Ravensbrück was an example of the chaos generated by a regime in the final months of defeat, a clearinghouse for the thousands of female prisoners arriving from the east. The rations doled out in Ravensbrück made the watery soup and stale bread of Auschwitz seem like a sumptuous feast. Many women survived on little else but melted snow.

If one was lucky enough to find a shelf to sleep on, it only had a quarter of the usual wooden slats across it necessary for support. It was like a comb missing most of its teeth. Many women were forced to sleep outside in the snow or on stable floors covered with muddy-puddled, lice-infested straw.

Survivor Hannah Cukier Horon recalled, "The barracks weren't ready for us, so they left us in the gutter, sleeping, peeing, and everything overnight. In the morning, we were frozen to the street, we couldn't even get up."[7]

Ravensbrück was a melting pot in the waning days of the war. Jewish prisoners were mixed with gentile political prisoners. Jewish former kapos, some who had treated their fellow Jews brutally in hopes of raising their own chances for survival, now shared the same circumstances as their former victims. One woman warned her former kapo that if she was around when they were set free, she would pay her back for all the beatings she had suffered.[8]

It was like the world had turned on its head. Some of the German guards, knowing the end was near and how harshly the world would judge them, almost kowtowed to the prisoners. "Suddenly [the Germans] weren't so bad to the Jews. Some would even tell us how good they had been [to us]. I was not used to this kind of behavior from the Germans," recalled Mala Liss.[9]

Edith Eisler Denes witnessed similar behavior from a guard as she, her sister, and her mother labored digging ditches in Ravensbrück. "Once, my mother was almost fainting, she couldn't do it, so a German—he wasn't an SS, but a German soldier who watched us—took it over and worked instead of her to finish her job."[10]

The fact that an ordinary German soldier and not an SS member was among the guards of a concentration camp in the final days of the war illustrates two things. First, the SS were abandoning their posts, knowing how culpable they were in carrying out the Final Solution. Secondly, the Third Reich was desperately low on manpower. Men were drafted into the Wehrmacht to fight battles or replace guards against their will, and for many, against their ideology. Sometimes in the last few months of the war, prisoners would experience the shock of a kind guard, as Edith Eisler Denes had. But this was still very much a rare exception. Most of the SS were brainwashed so completely that they were willing to fight and die for Hitler.

In Auschwitz, the women had set the rhythm of their days by work and food. In Ravensbrück, there was no work and virtually no food. If the women received food, there was no schedule to its distribution. They literally didn't know when their next meal was coming, or even *if* it was coming.

"We were there … a couple of weeks, not working, not doing anything. They [the Germans] had to think what to do with us. They were making our life miserable," said survivor Rose Frochewajc Mellender.[11] One popular activity to while away the hours was to pick lice off each of each other's bodies. Chaja and Surah spent two to three idle weeks in Ravensbrück before being transported to one of its many subcamps.

Flossenbürg was the fourth largest concentration camp in Germany. Situated in a small village in a beautiful forested area with mountain views, the location for Flossenbürg was chosen by Himmler himself due to its suitability for producing granite for Nazi construction projects. Flossenbürg was intended to house 1,600 inmates. By the time Szlama arrived, the main camp was overflowing with almost 14,500 prisoners.

Flossenbürg's first inmates, mainly criminals, "asocials," and homosexuals, arrived on May 3, 1938. Once the war started, the

German concentration camp Dachau was partially evacuated so it could be used as a training center for the future SS extermination squad, and 981 of its prisoners were transferred to Flossenbürg. Due to the increasing number of prisoners, Flossenbürg was constantly being transformed. On April 5, 1940, the first convoy of foreign prisoners arrived.

Living conditions in Flossenbürg were extremely cruel. The SS administration itself considered Flossenbürg as a "Hard Regime" concentration camp. Most of the prisoners had to work in the granite quarries. Thousands of them died of malnutrition, a total lack of hygiene and medical care, and from the violence of the SS guards.

Housing consisted of sixteen huge wooden barracks. The camp also had a kitchen, an infirmary, a laundry, and a disinfecting house. There were crematoria and an execution area located just beside the crematoria for "practical reasons," according to the SS. The whole camp was surrounded by an electrified, barbed-wire fence and watchtowers. Eventually, more than 111,000 prisoners would be incarcerated in Flossenbürg and its subcamps, and it is estimated that seventy-three thousand people lost their lives here.[12]

Survivor Fernand Van Horen recalled the following:

> The conditions of life are incredible. Nobody can imagine the bestiality and the cruelty of the SS guards. It is really hell here! And there are very few survivors of this hell! We entered a barrack and are immediately faced with what will be common for us in the next months; an inmate is beaten to death with a whip. We don't know the reason why this poor fellow is beaten to death. Torture, shootings, hangings, all of this is just normal life in Flossenbürg. The most common threat of the SS is "Krematorium". The day after our arrival in the camp, we are sent to a kommando: we must take huge stones on our back and transport it [sic] from one hill to another. Of course, we are beaten during

the whole day with clubs, rifles, etc. I soon realize
that we have no chance to survive from here![13]

Because of its distance from the front, Flossenbürg had been
selected as one of the camps that could accept death marchers. The
arrival of transports from the east led to a steep rise in the mortality
rate in the camp, with the peak month for mortality being February
1945, with an average of fifty-nine prisoner deaths a day. In the
pandemonium of a decaying guard system, many Russian prisoners,
thought to be escape or resistance risks, were selected for liquidation
before they were given the chance to attempt it.[14]

Up to this point, Szlama had survived by fortitude, determination,
street smarts, and more than a little luck. Now threatened with
starvation (some inmates were resorting to cannibalism), rampant
disease, and a system in complete breakdown, he would survive
Flossenbürg. But he would not remain there long enough to be
liberated from it.

TWENTY-FOUR

CHAPTER

During the two weeks that Chaja spent in Ravensbrück, there was a constant redistribution of prisoners. From 1944 on, most prisoners transported there were taken to one of its thirty-eight subcamps. Many women mistakenly felt that life in a subcamp would be safer, with less security and no gas chamber, but that wasn't the case.[1]

Chaja and Surah were transported one final time, by rail, to Neustadt-Glewe, located 130 kilometers farther west from the advancing Red Army and only a one-day ride from Ravensbrück.

When Chaja and Surah reached Neustadt-Glewe, the small camp had been in operation for only about six months, since September 1944. The mostly female prisoners fell into three major groups: Poles from the August 1944 Warsaw Ghetto uprising, Hungarians who had escaped extermination due to their usefulness to the armaments industry, and evacuees from Auschwitz like Chaja and Surah.

The prisoners in Neustadt-Glewe when Chaja and Surah arrived supplied slave labor to the nearby Dornier airplane factory. The aircraft factory was running at full capacity and needed no additional workers, so the newcomers were given nothing to do. The camp was totally unequipped for the arrival of its new inmates. Like Ravensbrück, many women had to wait days before they were fed. The influx of these women so late in the war stretched the camp, which had originally been built to house nine hundred prisoners, to a population of nearly five thousand by April 1945. Unlike Birkenau's living quarters, there were windows, but there were no bunks. Instead, the women slept on the ground on a thin layer of straw.[2] Another downgrade in conditions at Neustadt-Glewe was the hygiene situation. Livia Szabo-Krancberg, a prisoner with Chaja, later wrote, "In [Birkenau] we'd take a shower once in six weeks. We'd leave our filthy tatters there and return with clean tatters. In Neustadt-Glewe, we lacked these features."[3]

As a result, typhus spread through the camp. The stricken women were trucked to a shack on the outskirts of the camp and left to die. "The shack had 3-tiered bunk beds alongside two opposite walls. In the middle of the shack was a giant platform filled with dying and dead inmates. Every other day, a group of men would remove the dead and replace them with the dying from the bunk beds. Next to the only free wall were chamber pots so close to one another, they gave the appearance of being strung together. The pots overflowed with bloody bowel movements that spilled to the floor," recalled Ms. Szabo-Krancberg.[4]

The original housing barracks were reserved for the prisoners who still worked at the aircraft factory. The Dornier management wanted to make sure its laborers got sufficient sleep, so they were the only women who slept in beds.[5] Remnants of Nazi efficiency were still in effect even as the Third Reich was crumbling.

It is difficult to imagine the benchmark by which the guards chose who was unfit. Virtually all Neustadt-Glewe's prisoners, especially those dangerously enfeebled from their previous degradations and death marches, fit into this category. Conditions in the camp were inconsistent with the sustainability of life. Chaja joined a camp population of women who were being starved to death rather than gassed. "They didn't kill at Neustadt-Glewe. They let people die," said one survivor. Cut off from supplies so late in the war, Neustadt-Glewe received no rations. Those prisoners too weak or sick with the epidemics of typhus, tuberculosis, or dysentery were trucked back to Ravensbrück and murdered.[6]

When the barracks were filled to bursting, prisoners stayed in grossly overcrowded, unheated airplane hangars without beds or toilets. "There was no room to lie down. It was so crowded. And there the soup was plain water. And the piece of bread was like ... white bread toast ... so it was much worse—the food in Neustadt-Glewe—than it was in Ravensbrück. And the walls were covered with lice, like bedbugs. I put my head in Regina's lap, and she picked the lice, and that's how we spent the days. We had no water, no shower—the conditions were the worst of the worst of the worst," recalled survivor Fela Kolat.[7]

Chaja and Surah, in the mistaken belief that if they found some work to do, they would be eligible for something more substantial to eat, organized a crew to pick up airplane parts from wreckage that had crashed in the area. They were also ordered to dig trenches to hinder the Allied forces' advance. In her memoir, *Rena's Promise: A Story of Sisters in Auschwitz*, Rena Kornreich Gelissen wrote, "We marched through the middle of town to work. The townspeople come [sic] out of their shops and homes to spit at us as we pass. The hatred in their eyes is dismaying; we are not human beings to them, we are lower than dogs ... One would think the townspeople would be grateful for the work we do to protect them, but they spit at us that evening as well."[8]

Survivor Dina Strassberg, however, recalled a different tone from the soldiers: "I felt the German soldiers were speaking in a different tone. They knew something bad was coming." Occasionally they gave out cigarettes or pieces of bread to the women. Some began apologizing, claiming, "I didn't know what the Germans were going to do. I come from Austria. I'm not a German."[9]

Younger soldiers were desperately needed at the front, and the camp's younger guards were replaced by much older soldiers. Chaja thought the guards were so old the women could have taken over the camp, but they didn't attempt it because they didn't have any place to go.

A portion of these new guards were not Nazis and did not mistreat the prisoners. Survivor Rebecca Lissing recalled a time close to the end of the war when her thirst was so severe that her tongue felt like sandpaper. A barrel of water appeared, and she and a group of women threw themselves at it. Instead of eliciting gunshots, the guards found the scene so horrifying they cried.[10]

In the war's final days, some of Neustadt Glewe's SS began to flee the approaching Allies. Unfortunately, more stalwart members, determined to carry out Hitler's policies through the end, continued to brutalize the prisoners. Survivor Miriam Blumenstock Unreich remembered an SS guard who amused himself by launching his German shepherd at the women to "scratch and bite and snarl" at them.[11]

During appel on the morning of April 22, 1945, a large group of planes flew over the camp. The women craned their necks to the sky. One plane flew so low that they could see the pilot's face. Everyone agreed it was a British plane and that they were being photographed. The next day was Hitler's fifty-sixth birthday. To commemorate the day, a large group of Allied planes blew up the nearby airplane factory. Explosions went on for hours, but not even one spark fell on the camp. Hours after the planes had dispatched their payload and returned to their base, fuel and ammunition continued to blow up. All work in the airplane factory ceased after the bombing.[12]

A few days later, Chaja and Surah were among a group of women tasked with clearing rubble from a nearby airport. As the women walked from the camp to the cleanup sites, they saw white flags hanging from village homes, signifying Neustadt-Glewe's readiness to surrender.

As Allied victory drew inevitably closer, a group of guards visited the camp's laundry, carrying civilian clothes for cleaning and pressing by the prison's laundresses. While waiting for their garments, they said how good they had been to the Jews and how the other Germans were the mean ones. Mala Liss could hear the fear in their voices as they talked about the approaching Russians. "They talked about the great tragedy that had befallen their country. Listening to them, I wanted to grab one of them and shake him and say, 'The great disaster that befell your country? You're the ones who started this. Don't you remember?'"[13]

When their clothes were ready, the guards instructed that they be wrapped in paper so no one could see what they were carrying. They peeked out of the laundry doors to make sure nobody was looking, then crept back to their barracks to change out of their SS uniforms. Within minutes, dressed like ordinary townspeople, they hastily snuck out of the camp.[14]

TWENTY-FIVE

Sometime in early 1945, the R. Fuess Company's factory in southwest Berlin was bombed. Fuess produced measuring instruments for aircraft weaponry, deemed vitally necessary by the Luftwaffe. An empty textile factory in a town in Germany bordering Czechoslovakia was quickly identified as a suitable replacement and refitted with the mechanicals needed to continue making the instruments. Slave labor was needed to get the company up and running again. With just two months until defeat, a new Nazi concentration camp, Schönheide, the name of the town, was created and outfitted with fifty male prisoners, in addition to POWs and civilian slave laborers.

On February 21, 1945, the fifty inmates were plucked from Flossenbürg and moved to Schönheide. The Nazis still held to the misguided belief that this last-ditch effort could somehow impact the losing tide of the war.

Among this group of prisoners were twelve Poles, ten of whom were Jewish.[1] Szlama was one of those Polish Jews. So was an old Plonsk acquaintance of his named Yossel Tischman.

Although Szlama was doing important work for the Nazis, he and his fellow prisoners were still mistreated. According to one eyewitness, "A prisoner sat on the lavatory steps in the courtyard. [German plant manager Walter] Arlt went to him and argued with him that he should work. Because he refused he kicked him in the stomach. The next day, the man was no longer alive."²

Five weeks after Szlama arrived in Schönheide, the original group of fifty had shrunk to forty-eight. One had died, and one, a Czech, had escaped. By April 13, 1945, appel records listed forty-six of the original fifty present, although at that point, it is possible that at least six prisoners had died, as was recorded by a prisoner from Luxembourg named Albert Hommel on April 14, 1945. However, SS documents list only two fatalities in Schönheide. If one were to choose whom to believe, former prisoner Hommel would be the least likely to fabricate the number. Even so, most of the original prisoners who entered Schönheide with Szlama were still alive and accounted for. Records show that Szlama was still a prisoner as late as April 13, 1945, the day the camp was evacuated.³ The discrepancy is important in pinpointing the date Szlama became a free man.

Szlama lined up for appel on April 13. He tucked in his uniform and stood perfectly still, his hands at his sides and his head down. The SS guards began to walk the line, hitting this prisoner and yelling at that one.

But when they were done, Szlama saw different movements in the camp.

"What do you think they're doing?" he asked his neighbor.

"Don't know," the man said, quickly moving away.

"Line up!" the young SS guard shouted, his face red but his boots still shiny despite the mud. Szlama moved into a column, but the two men behind him were hit with a baton for not moving fast enough.

"March!"

And Szlama did. He took a deep breath. At least the weather was warmer, and the sun was out. At one time, shining sun inspired hope. But here, a rising sun just marked one day flowing into the next. But one took hope where one could find it.

Eight hours later, Szlama reached his destination: Johanngeorgenstadt. It didn't look any different from any other camp, but Szlama was tired. His legs hurt so much from the hard ground, and he desperately wanted to sit down. But he knew better than to try. Was there water? His mouth was so dry. He held little hope for this place.

"Halt! Turn around."

It took a minute for the command to set in. A minute and a few batons. Slowly Szlama and his fellow prisoners turned around and began to walk back toward Schönheide. Nothing they did made sense. But Szlama began to wonder just how bad things were going for Germany.

This march was documented by Albert Hommel, a Holocaust survivor, who wrote: "Camp Schönheide ... 43 prisoners arrived without losses via Eibenstock on 13.4.45, went back toward Schönheide, from where they were evacuated on the next day on orders from the local commanding officer ..."[4]

Not everything Hommel recorded was accurate. For instance, he claimed that a particularly cruel kapo, a gentile named Weilbach, was shot to death by a prisoner who then escaped with several others. However, Weilbach was sentenced to life in prison at the Flossenbürg trial after the war.

But Hommel was correct in one respect. During the resumed evacuation, there was an escape attempt by several of the prisoners on the road between Schönheide and the nearby town of Eibenstock on the day of the evacuation. Some prisoners were shot.[5] But it is highly likely that a few did escape. Indeed, the story Szlama told many years later juxtaposed well with Hommel's version.

TWENTY-SIX

Even as Neustadt-Glewe's guards were sneaking away, prisoner transports continued arriving until the end of April.[1] The women could hear Allied bombing close to the camp, but at this point, many of them were numb from the trauma they'd already experienced. Rebecca Lissing said she wasn't scared of being killed by bombardment. It would be a welcome way to die compared with being gassed.[2]

On the morning of May 2, 1945, with four thousand inmates locked in their barracks, most of Neustadt's guards snuck out of the camp in civilian clothes. When it was clear to the women that their captors had fled, they broke down the doors and window bars and stormed the kitchen, pouncing on the bread and potatoes that the Germans had hoarded.

One of those women, Wanda Poltawska, recalled, "A mob of screaming women [broke] into the stores and hurl[ed] themselves on to the food. Some of the weaker ones were being crushed underfoot ... They were snatching food from each other's grasp, pulling each other's hair, tearing each other's flesh with their nails. Blood flowed."[3]

The women made fires outside and began cooking the potatoes. If they'd had the opportunity in the past to steal a potato, it had been eaten raw.

Some of the women were openly joyful. But for others, the pain of what they had suffered and lost was too great for even liberation to assuage. For survivor Rivka Mincberg, who was left entirely without family and friends, liberation day was miserable. "I had nothing to rejoice over," she said.[4]

Alina Bacall-Zwirn broke into a storeroom, taking sugar, flour, and cigarettes. When she tried comprehending what was happening, "I went on top of the garbage dump and I looked out, and I thought, 'I'm going crazy.' I couldn't talk, I couldn't smile, I couldn't do nothing [sic]."[5]

Nearby was a newly liberated camp of male French POWs. They came to Neustadt-Glewe and disabled the electrified fence so the gate could be opened. Women who had been housed in barracks outside the perimeter of the fence liberated themselves by breaking through the doors and undoing the barbed wire outside their windows. The women could hardly believe they were free. Some who still had the energy began to dance.

Many women left the camp and returned with a US Army patrol in the area. However, Neustadt-Glewe was part of the Russian military zone, not the American zone, so the US Army had no jurisdiction to liberate the camp. They told the women that the Russians were close and would be there soon, and handed out chocolate and cigarettes. They left shortly after.[6]

Later that afternoon, Red Army tanks rolled in to formally liberate the camp, as well as the town of Neustadt-Glewe. The soldiers were visibly shaken by what they encountered. Many of the inmates were suffering from delirium. Another survivor remembered that by the time she was liberated, "Hunger didn't hurt anymore, but thirst was the worst."[7] The women who had gorged themselves with food began to get sick, and some died because their wasted bodies couldn't cope with the onslaught of fat and calories. Before they succumbed, they suffered horribly from stomach pains and diarrhea.

The Soviet soldiers told the women to move into the barracks that had been used by the Nazis so they could improve their living conditions. Survivor Fela Kolat theorized that the Soviets told the women to move into the barracks so they could take advantage of them. "Two Russian guys come [sic] in with a flashlight, shined us in the face," she recalled. "So [my friend] said, 'we are sick girls,' and this guy, maybe he was intelligent … he left us alone. The next day we had to take a piece of [metal] furniture. So where the door is, we put this outside so they would not see the door. We were afraid."[8]

Some of the women thought their emaciated condition (they weighed an average of sixty-six pounds) would be a deterrent to the Russian soldiers.[9] It was not.

Unfortunately, the women of Neustadt-Glewe were not alone in being raped upon liberation. Such behavior by Russian troops was extremely widespread. For some Jewish women across areas liberated by the Russians, their very moment of liberation was accompanied by simultaneous rape by the soldiers who had freed them.

The following illustrates the mind-set of many of the Russians: Russian liberators found a group of Jewish women hiding in a basement after they fled their camp while it was being heavily bombed. They began raping a woman named Ellen Getz. When the other prisoners tried to explain to them that this was a woman who had been a victim of the Nazis, the Russian soldiers simply replied, "A woman is a woman." According to the later testimony of one of the Russians, the common explanation was, "We set you free, so why not?" Many of the raped women contracted venereal diseases, and some became pregnant.[10]

As stories of survivor rape spread, women either hid or tried to stick together to be less vulnerable. Some tried to look sick and contagious when they learned of approaching Russian troops.[11]

Of course, not all Russians were rapists. Many were genuine liberators and were warmly received by the former prisoners.[12]

Chaja had mixed feelings about the Russian soldiers. She was so afraid of them that she would sleep in the troughs that horses ate out of, covered with straw, so the Russians wouldn't find her. She had a friend who became pregnant after being raped by a Russian soldier, and she hated them for that. Throughout her life, when someone brought up Russians, she would say "Javeushkas," which is the Russian word for "young woman." These experiences clearly tormented her. But freedom was something Chaja took seriously. She knew her immediate family had not survived. Other than her cousin, she knew no one else.

TWENTY-SEVEN

For the rest of his life, Szlama maintained that he had escaped from the last concentration camp he had been in, but he claimed to have jumped from the back of a truck along with some fellow prisoners returning to camp after a work detail. The story he told was that their guard, who was working alone that day, told them that they were to be liquidated immediately upon their return to camp, but he would not shoot at them if they attempted to run away. They jumped immediately.

Did Szlama change the story? Did he get so used to telling it that it became his truth? Perhaps he was on a truck and not on foot during his return to Schönheide after the initial evacuation of the camp. What is certain, though, is that Szlama did escape with one Yugoslav, one Hungarian, one Greek, his Plonsk acquaintance Yossel Tischman, and possibly others.[1] When telling the story later, Szlama always referred to all the others simply as "the Greeks."

As soon as the men jumped from the truck, one of them became the self-appointed leader. He pointed to the nearby woods and gestured for them to go in that direction, whispering, "Mono en linea" (Only one line). The Germans would have a harder time following a single line of footsteps than multiple tracks. That is, if the Nazis were even going to concern themselves with a few runaway Jews, with the Russians so close.

Szlama and Yossel, the only two Poles, stuck together at first. They were together in the same group, but it was by chance, not by choice. The two Plonskers had known each other most of their lives, though they'd never been particularly close. Yossel didn't want to stay with the group and struck out on his own, as did the Hungarian and the Yugoslavian. Yossel did not want Szlama to come with him, saying it was safer if he was alone. He disappeared into the woods.[§]

Szlama had another reason for wanting to remain with Yossel: If he died alone in the woods, no one would know that he had passed. There would be no one to say Kaddish for him, the Jewish prayer for the dead.

Yossel's decision left Szlama with the other men, the "Greeks," who reluctantly allowed him to stay. They seemed to be able to understand one another, probably speaking a Sephardic dialect (ethnic Jewish culture originating from southeastern Europe and North Africa). Whatever language it was, Szlama wasn't familiar with it. But he sensed that they seemed to know where some partisan huts might be located, information they may have received from some of the gentile Polish prisoners.

Whether there were huts or not, the group didn't find them by nightfall. They covered themselves with leaves and brush and settled in for the long, cold night.

The next few days yielded more wandering and nothing else. The Greeks, perhaps out of frustration, expelled Szlama from the group. It wasn't that he couldn't keep up with them; he just wasn't one of them. He was outnumbered and couldn't speak their language. They had safe houses identified by other Greeks, as well as food, but Szlama would always mean more work to understand what they were going to do and more risk because he stood out. He had no option but to set off by himself. Aside from losing his family, it was his worst

---

[§] The two men stayed in touch throughout their lives, even attending the Bar Mitzvahs of each other's sons. Szlama never confronted Yossel about his decision to go out on his own.

fear realized, but he understood the separation was a matter of safety and not personal.

Faced with the isolation, Szlama soon realized that there were benefits to being free of the Greeks. Gone was the worry of trying to fit in, to not make a misstep that would displease them. He hadn't really wanted to be with them anyway. What he had wanted was to go off with Yossel.

Szlama had always been resourceful and clever. He just had to tap into those qualities, be the man who had walked to Bialystok and back undetected; the man who had managed to survive one of the longest death marches of the war, a sadistic medical experiment, a broken collarbone, starvation, beatings. Alone in the woods, he could survive, so long as he wasn't caught. No one was torturing him. He was free to scavenge for whatever food he could find. He didn't have to bend to anyone else's will.

But there was one huge drawback to the solitude. In the silence, there was no diversion from his emotional suffering. The intense loneliness he felt wandering in the woods was like a physical pain crushing him from every direction. *If I die alone in the woods, what was the meaning of my life?* he thought. He spent hours reflecting on his life and his lost family, wondering what the point of any of it had been. If he died, there would be no record that he had *lived*. Doubt flooded him. Maybe he should have stayed in the camp where, if he died, there might have been some record of it. If anyone he knew survived, perhaps they would have looked for him and learned of his death.

Still, his ruminations in the woods stirred something else in him. His mantra in the camps, "Another day, another day," returned, and with it came a little grit, and then a little more. He had withstood so much already. Perhaps he was meant to survive, after all, and build back his life. His past was dead. But he *could* have a future. The war was almost over. If he could just hang on a little longer, he could try to recapture some meaning to his life.

Once Szlama made the decision to keep going, he formulated a plan. He knew the Russians were moving west toward Germany. He could hear the bombs they were dropping to clear their way. So he followed the sounds of the explosions, hoping to get to the Russian front. A catch-22 of following the bombardment was that, ironically, he could be killed by it. Also, if the planes were dropping bombs, the Germans were in the area, and he needed to avoid them and their checkpoints. If he was unlucky enough to encounter Nazis, he decided, he would assume the identity they expected, that of a dumb Polak, head bowed, looking off to the side.

He trekked southeast toward Czechoslovakia, staying in the camouflage of the woods. Hopefully Czechoslovakia would be liberated by the time he got there—if he got there. Then he would finally be free.

TWENTY-EIGHT

CHAPTER

Chaja's cousin Surah was one of the women to storm the kitchen for food that morning in the spring of 1945. Unbeknownst to her, there were still a few German holdouts in the camp. They were either Neustadt-Glewe guards or Wehrmacht soldiers hiding in the camp during their retreat from the front. When the women broke down the kitchen doors, there were shots fired. Some women were killed at the very moment they were freed. Surah's leg was grazed by a bullet. Her hysteria was so great that she thought her entire leg had blown off. She hopped on one leg to the barracks where Chaja was waiting, screaming, "I lost my leg! I only have one leg!" Despite her agitation, she still managed to clutch the piece of bread she had obtained before being shot. Chaja looked at her cousin like she was crazy and shouted back, "No you don't! You have both of your legs!"

Both women showed incredible fortitude in the next few days, dovetailing each other's personal strengths. Chaja cooked food for them both, doling it out little by little so they wouldn't get sick. Whatever she cooked, it must have tasted wonderful in comparison to the potato skins they'd been stealing from the garbage.

The Russians told the healthiest women to go to the stores and homes in town and take as much food as they could carry. Surah, being the more outspoken of the two, made the trip after she had regained enough strength, demanding food from all the German civilians she encountered. When the townspeople hesitated, Surah boldly threatened to find a Russian or American soldier who would make them hand it over. The threat worked. The Germans complied. Some of the women did even better, taking over the homes of local Germans who'd recently fled Neustadt-Glewe.

During the next few nights, the cousins split up. Chaja slept in the horses' water trough, covering herself with straw. Surah chose the kitchen. Each woman believed *her* choice was the safest. The decision to separate at night illuminates the relationship between the two cousins. They still weren't emotionally close, even after surviving the Holocaust together. One thing was certain, however. Surah and Chaja, not knowing if anyone else in their extended family had survived, would leave the camp *together*.

Physically bolstered by the addition of vegetables and tinned meat to their diet, the cousins were ready to leave within a few days. In preparation for their journey, Surah walked to a nearby farm, feeling entitled enough to take a horse and wagon and return with it to the camp. Joining Surah and Chaja were a Plonsk woman named Neha and a few other women. It was so effortless, too outlandish to be believed, that these female survivors would be able to simply ride their wagon inviolably through the wasteland of Europe.

Predictably, Russian soldiers confiscated their horse almost immediately. Undeterred, the women continued east on foot, once again stopping at homes to demand food from the Germans, threatening to bring Allied soldiers to those who didn't willingly hand it over. At night, they slept in barns. Eventually, they reached a train station where they met two Jewish soldiers from Łódź who invited them to ride to Warsaw and kindly shared their food. It didn't matter that the women didn't have any money, because the trains were running for free. As Chaja watched skeletons of towns and cities ravaged by Hitler pass by her window, she scarcely believed she had survived. She and Surah rode all the way to Praga, a district of Warsaw located on the east bank of the Vistula River. Unlike the razed western parts of Warsaw, Praga had been relatively untouched.

There, the International Red Cross gave them much-needed assistance in the form of food, clothing, and shelter (the floor of a large room with about one hundred others). They stayed for two days, then decided to make the short trip to Zakroczym, hoping for the slim chance they might find surviving family members. Additionally, Chaja's parents had left some belongings with a goyim neighbor, and she was determined to reclaim them. Instead of a warm welcome, however, the patriarch of the goyim family, once considered enough of friend to be trusted with their possessions, opened the door with a shocked expression.

Once he'd regained his voice, he said sarcastically, "Lucky us. All the other Jews were killed, and people got to keep their stuff, but you came back."

Chaja didn't know what to say.

He said, "Wait here," and shut the door.

After about ten minutes, he pushed a few photographs through a small opening in the door. He acted as if she was stealing them from him at gunpoint.

"There are yours," he said.

She reached to take them, and no sooner had she pulled her hand back than the door was slammed shut.

Chaja turned away quickly. There wasn't anything of value; the Friedmans had never owned anything extravagant. But the family photographs were the only vestiges of Chaja's previous life and the people she had loved. And they were all she had left.

Based on the hostile reception Chaja, Surah, and the other few returning Jews in Zakroczym were receiving, they decided to go to Plonsk, a larger town where Chaja might find people she'd known from her ghetto days. Surely a more sizable town would yield more survivors. There would be strength in numbers.

Chaja and Surah were following the trajectory of most survivors, first returning to their hometowns, and upon finding no or almost no survivors, continuing to the last homes they'd lived in before the war—the ghettos they'd been forced to inhabit. Widening the search from family members to family *and* ghetto friends raised the chances of finding *someone* they'd known before the war. "Maybe we'd find someone," said Surah years later. "Maybe a miracle."[1]

The two cousins hopped a train for the short ride to Plonsk.

TWENTY-NINE

After days of stumbling through the forest, Szlama came to a clearing. He saw a barn, a small house, and a wooden outbuilding. He could hear animals in the barn, so he knew the house was inhabited. He stayed behind the tree line long enough to ascertain that the woman he'd seen going back and forth to the barn lived alone. There was no trace of anyone else on the property—no men's clothing on the clothesline hanging beside her stockings. He could wait until nightfall and creep to the barn to look for food and a place to sleep, but he was too hungry to wait that long. It had been days since he'd eaten anything. The woman was alone, he reassured himself. She'd probably be more frightened of him than he had reason to be of her, unless she had Nazi friends in the area. Still, the clearing seemed remote, and Szlama decided to take his chances. He approached the front door to the house and knocked softly. He was terrified but tried to appear calm.

The woman answered the door, showing no fear. There was nothing threatening about the filthy, smelly, skeletal figure at her door. To her credit, she didn't register any revulsion either. Szlama asked her if she spoke Polish. He was in Germany, but the borders had changed so many times there was a good chance that she was ethnically Polish. When she responded that she did, the words rushed from his mouth.

"I am a Polish citizen," he said. "I just escaped from a concentration camp where I was imprisoned for being a Socialist. I lost my wife and daughter. I'm alone. My whole family is dead. I need a place to hide and papers to prove I'm a citizen so I can walk freely through German checkpoints without being suspected as a Jew. I need a place to stay, and I need food. I can work."

The woman was instantly empathetic. "My husband—he's away at the front. But we're both ethnic Poles," she said, ushering him in. "I haven't heard from him in many months." She opened her door wider and told him to hurry in; there were German patrols in the area.

After he entered the house, she told him they owned the small mill, and she had animals that needed feeding. Szlama would have plenty of work to do to earn his keep.

Szlama had left his own home for the Plonsk Ghetto on May 16, 1941. It was now April 1945. He looked around the room. It was stark and utilitarian: a sink, a wooden table, two chairs, a stove, a large woodpile, some pots, and a few cooking utensils. It was the most beautiful place he had ever seen.

The woman gestured for him to take a seat at the table, and she quickly ladled soup from the pot on the stove and set it before him. The smell was intoxicating. He put his hands around the bowl, reveling in its warmth, and realized that he hadn't eaten anything hot since the noodles he'd filched while fattening the geese in Birkenau. He spooned the soup into his mouth slowly and purposefully, being mindful of not gulping it down. When the bowl was empty, the woman immediately refilled it, sitting down to join him at the table.

They talked quietly about the ordeals they'd faced during the war.

"My husband is off fighting. I'm running the lumber business myself," the woman said. "I have no idea if he's still alive."

Szlama didn't see any evidence of her having any children, and he decided he would be as honest with her as possible about his experiences in the camps. He told her about the various placed in which he'd been imprisoned, the forced labor, the viciousness of the guards, the starvation rations. The only thing he omitted was that he was a Jew.

She listened quietly, letting out small sympathetic murmurs from time to time. When Szlama finished speaking, she went to the pump, filled her biggest pot with water, and placed it on the stove. When the water was boiling, she poured it into a steel tub and added some cool water to it. From a cupboard, she retrieved a towel and a small cake of homemade soap. When she retreated, Szlama removed his grungy rags and lowered himself into the water, luxuriating in the sensation. He scrubbed himself until he was red and raw, as if trying to shed his top layer of skin. When he was satisfied, he toweled off. The woman had thoughtfully left some clothes belonging to her husband on one of the chairs.

The next day, she started a fire in the yard and burned Szlama's old clothes.

Szlama stayed with the woman for about a week and a half. After a few days spent sleeping in the barn under heavy wool blankets and eating three nourishing meals a day, his strength was restored to the point that he could help with woodcutting and caring for the animals. With each bath, bowl of steaming, hearty soup, and the new clothes, Szlama felt like he was being reborn. He could hardly believe his good fortune, but he knew his situation was still precarious. The war was not over, and without papers, he was not safe. And he was putting his benefactor at risk too. If the local Gestapo came to her home, they would both be shot.

Mercifully, Szlama's reversal of fortune continued. The woman had some contacts in the Home Army Resistance who procured official identity documents for him that were so convincing they even had a swastika stamped on the front.

He looked at them with amazement, the officialness of them. The security, freedom, they offered.

It was a daunting prospect to leave the safety of the snug little cabin. The end of the war couldn't be far off. If his papers were authentic enough, he'd be safe even if the Nazis appeared at the door. But Szlama was anxious to leave German territory, and he knew he had to do so soon. During his time with the woman, he had experienced the feeling of freedom, but he wasn't truly free—not in Germany.

When Szlama set out a couple of weeks later, he was well nourished, clean, decently dressed, with solid documents. But he was still extremely vulnerable. If he encountered a suspicious German brazen enough to order him to drop his pants, his circumcision would instantly betray him as a Jew. The inner drive that had pushed him for so long, however, propelled him forward. He needed to travel southeast all the way into Czechoslovakia. His strategy was to again head toward the sounds of bombardment and the Russian front.

Szlama had been walking only a short time before his biggest fear was realized. He was stopped at a German checkpoint. The long pole was set across the road with a Gestapo wagon off to the side, with at least two Nazis inside. Two Nazis in full Nazi attire held machine guns, and German shepherds came forward, from around the truck, waiting eagerly.

Because he wasn't anywhere near a main road, it came as a shock. He immediately assumed the demeanor the Nazis expected of a Pole, based on their prejudicial belief in self-superiority. He slouched, casting his head down and off to the side.

"Papers!" the soldier barked. All the soldiers began to gather nearby.

Szlama handed them over without a word and looked down.

The soldier snatched the papers and said, "I wonder if he's a *fafluchte* Jude (fucking Jew)." The other soldiers laughed.

Szlama knew his papers were inscrutable, but only the thin fabric of his pants separated him from a bullet to the back of the head. To his horror, the Nazis began to discuss whether they should make him drop his trousers before they ultimately decided it would be in poor taste. Ripping babies in half was acceptable. Locking entire populations of towns into buildings and burning them alive was acceptable. Asking a man to drop his pants—that was indefensible. This absurd Nazi etiquette saved Szlama's life.

"Go," the solider said, handing him his papers.

Szlama took them without looking up and shuffled through the checkpoint.

It was miles before his heart resumed its normal rhythm.

A few hours later, he ran into another group of Germans, though this time they were, thankfully, deceased. He walked around them. There were six, a mix of young and old, their bodies positioned in a way that indicated they died where they fell. No one had bothered to move them out of the way.

He took a few more steps back and listened intently. He didn't hear anything that indicated any of the unit was nearby. He knew they'd be carrying valuables he'd need to trade.

He waited a few more minutes. His decision was made, and his action swift. He rifled through the dead soldiers' pockets and rucksacks, finding food, a compass, and gold watches. He put a few watches on his wrists and pocketed everything else he could eat or trade. He left their weapons behind. Szlama hated guns and had no desire to ever fire one, even in self-defense.

Lying near the dead Germans was a bicycle. It was another stroke of luck, another sign that perhaps he really was meant to survive. Szlama had always loved bikes. He hopped on and rode, a bit wobbly at first but soon gaining momentum. It was a huge improvement from walking. As he rode, he encountered more and more dead Germans, stopping every time to take anything of value, even discarding his bicycles for better models several times.

When he crossed the border into Czechoslovakia, he was the owner of nine gold watches. He had literally gone from rags to riches. What's more, the Russian soldiers in Czechoslovakia greeted him as a comrade. Szlama didn't know how to respond to such a rapid change in circumstances. It was an unimaginable experience, going from someone whose life had no value to this newfound freedom and goodwill. He was surrounded by people who also had the Germans as enemies, men who had lost but now had won. For the first time in a long time, he felt no fear.

He literally felt the hairs on his scalp stand on end, a tingling all over his body. Years later, reminiscing of that day, he said, "You know, something like this could make you meshuga," (Yiddish for crazy). The powerful emotions laid bare by the instant transition from years of indescribable suffering to immediate liberation were almost more than he could cope with. He'd survived hell. Now he had to relearn how to live while forever shouldering the burdens of his physical and mental scars.

At first, the Russians were very nice to him. They shared their vodka and bread with him as well as their own accounts of terrible loss—their sisters being raped and killed, their families and homes destroyed by the Germans. These were stories Szlama could understand because he'd learned enough Russian during his year in Bialystok to communicate in the language. He reciprocated, sharing with them the murders of his brothers, half sisters, stepmother, wife, and daughter. He told of his years in the ghetto and the camps, the agony of the death march. They listened with sympathy, bonded to him through their shared hatred of the Nazis. But when the Russians got drunk, they turned belligerent. "We lost our families, too, and we liberated you, so give us three of your watches," they said, pointing their rifles at him. Reluctantly, he did as they asked.

He stayed with them for two or three days before he thought better of it. Eventually, he was taken care of by an empathetic Czech family, who gave him a room to stay in their house. The Czechs had heard of the atrocities Szlama had withstood without him having to speak of them. They treated him kindly, feeding him and providing him with clothing. It was another abrupt departure from his status of only the previous month. Even more extraordinary, Czech homes had modern plumbing. Szlama had never seen the luxury of an indoor toilet before, much less the running water with hot and cold spigots found in the kitchens *and* the bathrooms. Many Czech households even had their own automobiles. Szlama thought he was in paradise, but he still longed to return to Plonsk to search for surviving friends and family, so he only stayed with them for about five days.

Western Czechoslovakia was formally liberated on May 9, 1945, but Szlama had moved on by then.[1] With his remaining watches and bicycle, he boarded a train for home.

THIRTY

Through the entirety of the war, only that one bomb, in September 1939, had fallen on Plonsk, landing smack in the center of the village square. All the town's buildings were intact, except for those that had been part of the ghetto. The Nazis had razed the ghetto after the last transport left for Auschwitz.

Chaja arrived by train, returning to a town remarkably similar, at least in appearance, to the one she had left in December 1942. Of the two cousins, Chaja had known more people, having spent more time in the ghetto, so she stood a better chance of knowing other returning Jews. She had been acquainted with several of the younger Baijgel brothers, particularly Itchele. She'd been intimidated and captivated by him, recalling that he had eyes "that could burn your eyes out." Perhaps she had carried some affection for him. Itchele *had* been the playboy of the family. At the very least, they had been friends.

As she encountered survivors in Plonsk, she would ask them if they saw Itchele. They hadn't, but they would mention they found Szlama in Plonsk.

Eventually, she encountered Szlama himself because all of them had returned to the Plonsk ghetto, which was about one square kilometer.

That encounter was the first time they had ever met, partly because Szlama had spent a year in Bialystok, and partly because he'd been an older, married father living separately from his brothers during their time in the ghetto.

Szlama had returned to Plonsk knowing that none of his brothers had survived, but he was happy to be reunited with his first cousins Meyer Fuks (later changed to Fox when he came to Ellis Island) and Meyer's sister Devorah, and Devorah's husband, Isach. He also was happy to see Hymie Pass, Srul Eisenburg, and Abba Lezerovitz.

Yossel Tischman had also survived, but the pain of leaving him with the Greeks when they escaped was still present for Szlama. Though Szlama hadn't known Chaja before the war, the fact that she had known his brothers brought him an immediate degree of comfort with her. Attaching himself to the group was another native Plonsker named Chaim Pass.

Szlama quickly became the de facto leader by finding the eight of them an empty house in the goyim section of the town. Szlama, Chaim, Hymie, and Devorah were Plonsker. Chaya, Abba, and Surah were Zacrocyner.

A daily domestic routine soon followed. Szlama rode his bike to the farmers he'd associated with before the war and either sold or traded his watches, one at a time, for fowl, carrots, potatoes, and onions. Whatever excess food he had, Szlama sold to other survivors. Chaja became the female head of the household, with the others assisting her. Surah didn't like the living arrangements, so she moved in with a formerly wealthy Jew who had been able to get his home and business back. He employed Surah as his maid, but she still maintained her relationship with the group. She grew especially close to Chaim Pass, whom she eventually married.

Szlama protected Chaja, Surah, and Devorah from the Russians. As with other areas they liberated, Red Army soldiers were still raping women. One night, a drunk Russian showed up at the group's home demanding sex.

Szlama shouted, "You want a hole?"

When the Russian responded affirmatively, Szlama took a hammer and smashed a hole in the wall. "Here's a hole for you!" he shouted.

The Russian left.

Szlama soon diversified his food runs to include the town's mill and dairy farms, where he procured bread, milk, eggs, and cheese. Szlama had always been a wheeler and dealer, and making money was his talent. His friends were well fed. In fact, they had more food than they needed.

One night, after the evening meal had been cleaned, Szlama joined Chaja in the kitchen. The quiet seemed to settle them both.

"I have more milk for tomorrow," he said.

"Sell it to the Plonskers. We've got all we need," Chaja replied.

Szlama smiled. He could always count on her. He leaned forward. "I can get more. Much more. I think it's time to start going to Berlin."

Chaja nodded. They had discussed this before. The food shortage meant Berliners would need—and pay for—what Szlama could provide. The trains were controlled by Russians, but they ran often and were relatively safe. There were dangers, of course, but advantages too for traveling as a couple.

"When do we leave?" she asked. Chaja was gutsy. She wasn't the least bit afraid to accompany him to Berlin. He admired her bravery.

The Battle of Berlin, fought from April 16 to May 2, 1945 (also known as the Fall of Berlin), was the final major European offensive of World War II. Adolf Hitler had already committed suicide on April 30, just before the decisive Allied victory. On May 7, the German High Command surrendered all its forces unconditionally, and May 8, 1945, was officially proclaimed V-E Day.[1] Berlin was nearly decimated. Many of the buildings still standing were no more than hollowed shells. An estimated 125,000 civilians were killed during the operation.[2] Virtually all transport to and from the city was inoperative. Bridges were destroyed; streets were covered in rubble. Bombed-out sewers had contaminated the city's water supply. Berliners were living like rats, scurrying about to find food, shelter, and water. For the women, there were the mass rapes by their Russian liberators to contend with. An estimated one hundred thousand women were raped after the conquest of Berlin.³ The mentality of the Russians in Berlin was in nefarious contrast to the Russians who raped because they felt it was their due as liberators of prisoners. The Russians in Berlin *hated* the Germans, and raping their women was about revenge.⁴

Berliners were starving and vulnerable, and the city was fertile ground for Szlama and Chaja to make money. They wasted no time in boarding a train to sell their food for the dollars, pounds, rubles, marks, and gold coins that were currently of no value to the hungry Berliners. What they needed most was something they could eat.

Szlama and Chaja were so successful in their dealings that they were soon scoring more money and jewelry than they could hide during their return train trips to Plonsk. Chaja started wearing a girdle so she could stuff more currency into it, but even the extra fortification couldn't hide how much she was carrying. Russian soldiers began to ask her how she could be so far along in her pregnancy so soon after the war. She used their inquiry to her advantage, no longer trying to hide the bump but making it bigger. This decoy saved her later.

She and Szlama had begun the practice of carrying bread with them, not to sell but to carry the surplus valuables. They cut the loaves in half, scooped them hollow, and glued them back together with egg yolk. Returning to Plonsk once, a Russian soldier demanded that Chaja hand over all her bread, grabbing it out of her hands. Chaja responded, "Can't you see I'm pregnant? I need to eat." Sheepishly, the soldier handed back a loaf of rye. But the valuables were in the pumpernickel, not the rye. Thinking quickly, Chaja said, "No. I want the pumpernickel. It's more nutritious." Luckily, he handed it over and accepted the rye in its place. Chaja and Szlama had the same instincts and were quite a team.

THIRTY-ONE

CHAPTER

Szlama and Chaja were living a life of plenty, both in food and material goods. If they were hearing about acts of violence against returning survivors in Poland, it didn't discourage them enough to leave the country. Business was too good in Berlin. Then in July, Szlama learned something deeply disturbing.

Szlama arrived at the small farm early in the morning. As agreed, the potato farmer was waiting for him in the barn.

"Hello," Szlama called. "How's it going today, Mendel?"

"It's good," he replied. But his normally jolly face was pale. He picked up a sack of potatoes and looked at Szlama expectantly.

Szlama showed him what he had to trade, but then he stopped. "What's wrong?" he asked. Caring about customers was good for business. The more people trusted you, the more they were willing to trade with you. But they became friends also, and information was a valuable commodity, just as food and water.

"In Nowy Dwor, just thirty-three kilometers from Plonsk, four survivors were hanged by gentile Poles in the town square. My wife's brothers were among them."

Szlama nodded, trying to cover the panic he now felt. His stomach hurt, and he felt a little dizzy. "Were there any others?"

"Yeah," Mendel said. "Riva Fuks."

Riva!

Szlama was badly shaken by the news. It was a brutally hot day, but he had suffered far worse than the bicycle ride he made in the heat to Nowy Dwor that day. When he arrived in the town, Riva and the three other victims were still swinging from their nooses. Szlama immediately cut their bodies down and buried them in graves he dug in the desecrated Jewish cemetery. He said Kaddish for them and rode back to Plonsk.

He burst into the home, shutting the door behind him. As soon as he saw Chaja, he said, "We're leaving."

"We're leaving?"

Then he told her what had happened. He didn't need to say much more. After the growing season, in October or November, there wouldn't be much to trade, and it would be the perfect time to go.

It was the right decision. In cities and towns throughout Poland, returning Jews were fleeing from their former homes due to the hostile "welcomes" they were receiving. With the passage of time, it became clear that the violence was not going to dissipate.

Traditional anti-Semitism nourished by the recent wave of annihilation, and fears that surviving Jews would demand the return of their property, led to regular pogroms (organized massacres). From 1945 to 1947, between one thousand and two thousand Jews lost their lives, more than in the decade before the war.[1] The most violent pogrom, which occurred in Kielce, Poland, on July 4, 1946, claimed at least forty-seven lives.[2]

Before that day, roughly 70 percent of Kielce's Jews lived in a building at 7 Planty Street, located in the center of town. Three days before the pogrom, an eight-year-old Polish boy named Henryk Błaszczyk was reported missing by his father, Walenty. The boy, who had gone to a nearby village without his parents' permission, returned home claiming that he'd been kidnapped, in the hopes he would avoid being punished. Henryk pointed to a nearby man, who happened to be a Jew, and said that he was the man who held him against his will in a cellar. His parents brought him to the police station, where Henryk repeated the same story. A police patrol of more than a dozen men were commanded to search the apartment building at 7 Planty Street, where the Jew lived. The police spread news of the supposed kidnapping and, to stir up further unrest against the Jews, told the gathering civilian crowd that they would also be searching for the bodies of other Polish children that the Jews may have ritually murdered.

News of the tension in Kielce reached the Polish army, the Interior Security Corps, and Polish military intelligence and counterintelligence agencies. They reacted to the news by sending about one hundred soldiers and five officers, who reached 7 Planty Street by ten o'clock in the morning. The soldiers hadn't been briefed on why they were dispatched, so they questioned the townspeople, who were stirred into such a frenzy that they were throwing rocks at the building. The soldiers then broke into the building to search for the kidnapped children, of course not finding any. In fact, the building did not even have a cellar. That fact did nothing to deter the Poles from forcing the Jews to surrender their valuables and their weapons, which they were licensed to have. No one knows who fired the first shot, but it was exactly the catalyst the Poles needed. Several people on both sides of the conflict were shot.

The fight moved outside, with the Jews being forced out of the building to a hail of rocks and sticks. By noon, as many as one thousand workers from a nearby steel mill arrived to conduct the next phase of the pogrom. They beat about twenty Jews to death with steel rods and clubs. No military or security commanders called for a halt in the attacks. Another police unit arrived, and rather than intervene, the officers joined the looting and violence, which continued inside and outside the building. The killing spread past 7 Planty Street when a young mother and her three-year-old son were taken from their home on a nearby street, robbed, driven out of the city, and shot.

The pogrom finally ended at approximately three o'clock in the afternoon with the arrival of a new unit of security forces and additional troops from Warsaw. Still, some injured Jews were further beaten and robbed while being transported to an area hospital, as well as *in* the hospital by fellow patients. A crowd of Poles even approached one hospital, demanding that the wounded Jews be handed over. The hospital staff refused.

Even trains passing through Kielce's railway station were searched for Jews, resulting in at least two passengers being shot or thrown off their train. Train killings reportedly continued for months after the pogrom, resulting in as many as thirty more murders likely instigated from the original event.[3]

In the three months following the Kielce pogrom, more than seventy-five thousand Jews fled Poland as part of a mass westward migration, knowing they had no future in their country of birth. "It can frankly be stated that eighteen months after the liberation, the war is not yet over for European Jewry," stated a report on Jewish Refugees and Displaced Person in Europe.[4]

Chaja and Szlama decided that the trips to Berlin would continue for the summer, and the couple would squirrel away as much money as possible.

THIRTY-TWO

From 1945 to 1952, more than 250,000 Jewish displaced persons (DPs) lived in camps and urban centers in Germany, Austria, and Italy. These facilities, colloquially called DP camps, were administered by the Allied authorities and the United Nations Relief and Rehabilitation Administration (UNRAA). Jewish survivors called themselves *She'erit Hapletah*, meaning spared remnant, a term traced back to the book of Ezra in the Hebrew Bible.[1]

In the months following the war's end in Europe, food was in short supply for the Germans, especially in large cities like Berlin where there was no agriculture to augment the shortage. The refugees and survivors in the DP (displaced persons) camps, however, had plenty to eat.

German citizens also had no way to make a living, unless they were lucky enough to procure jobs as cooks or workers in the DP camps. They were willing to barter almost anything, such as watches, jewelry, precious stones, and gold, to obtain the food, cigarettes, chocolate, coffee, and toiletries that were in healthy supply to the DPs. Conversely, since the well-fed DPs lacked many of the extra necessities, such as warm winter outerwear, sturdy shoes, and boots that many Germans possessed, the stage was set for the black market to flourish.[2]

The Jewish DP police, not the German police, had the responsibility of enforcing laws in the DP camps. They maintained law and order in Zeilsheim and guarded the camp's perimeter; they kept their own house in order. The Jewish camp police were impressive proof of the success of self-government. An ordinance issued by the camp administration laid out their rights and responsibilities. The police department was defined as the division of the camp administration responsible for safety and order. It consisted of a criminal investigation section, a constabulary, an emergency medical team, and a firefighting brigade. The police were permitted to detain anyone charged with the commission of a crime, or whom they believed guilty of having committed a crime, for twenty-four hours. To keep a suspect in custody any longer, they had to seek authorization from the camp court. The police could also obtain warrants to search residences or other places for stolen goods and to confiscate any if they were found.

One of the most important and complicated tasks facing the Jewish police—a task that also confronted the German police—was fighting the black market.

Jews were as equally involved in black market activities as the Germans and members of the American military government. Black marketeering was rampant in Germany after the war, and it was certainly illegal.[3] Why didn't the Jewish police look the other way when Zeilsheim residents, given what they'd suffered at the hand of the Germans, participated in the black market? In the opinion of survivor Arno Lustiger, they should have. "You have to know that we (survivors) got necessary foodstuffs, but nothing else. Everything else … from combs to shoes, you had to get by trading. The Jews had nothing to trade, while the Germans could at least trade their property."[4]

Jewish police cracked down on Jewish black marketeers because they feared that the criminal activities of a few might reflect negatively on the entire Jewish community. Accusations of black marketeering contributed greatly to reviving the ancient stereotypes of the Jew as a trader and haggler, incapable of pursuing a real occupation.

These prejudices were fostered, on the one hand, by the traditional aversion that many Germans felt toward Eastern European Jews, whom they regarded as quintessentially alien, and on the other, by their dependency on the Jews for the material goods that they received from the US Army and the UNRAA.[5]

Some Jewish DPs did refuse to work. The American army, demonstrating a complete lack of sensitivity, tried to compel them to labor in areas that benefited the community at large. The army thought the DPs "shouldn't loaf around without work, but should participate in the construction of the German economy," remembered Arno Lustiger. "That was an [unfathomable] idea that we should help the Germans build their economy, when they themselves destroyed it with their own guilt and their own crimes."[6]

THIRTY-THREE

Szlama and Chaja had learned of the DP camps during their regular trips into Germany. One of them, Zeilsheim, near Frankfurt, seemed to have better accommodations than the others. Zeilsheim, the Red Cross DP camp located in Frankfurt am Main, Germany, was in the American Zone. Szlama and Chaja, Devorah and Meyer Fuks, Devorah's husband, Shachna, Chaim Pass, and Surah entered Zeilsheim on November 8, 1945.

The Allies' first responsibilities were to bring some order to everyday life amid the chaos of postwar Germany and to find living quarters for the DPs. There were more than 140,000 Jewish DPs in the US Zone camps following the surge of Jews who fled Poland.[1] Jewish relief organizations furnished the survivors with financial support, medical aid, and critically needed psychotherapy, for which they were ill-equipped. Most of the refugees suffered from psychological difficulties after the devastating traumas they had experienced and witnessed. They were often distrustful and apprehensive around authorities. Gradually, however, the military authorities of the three Western Allies (American, Russian, and British) began to understand the unique problems facing the Jewish DPs.

Living quarters in the DP camps varied according to what was available in each location: barracks, former POW and slave labor camps, industrial workers' housing, tent cities, hotels, apartment buildings, garages, stables, monasteries, hospitals, sanitariums, schools, and so on.[2]

Zeilsheim, officially opened on August 22, 1945, was one of the largest DP camps in Germany, with a population of more than three thousand by the end of December 1945. The number would grow. Aside from its size, Zeilsheim differed from other DP camps because it was one of the only camps where Occupation forces requisitioned hundreds of German civilians' homes, formerly brick workers' barracks from I. G. Farben, to house the DPs. In an ironic reversal, workers for the company that had produced Zyklon B were forcibly removed from their homes so that Jews who had been spared the gas chambers could move in.

The swap in housing from German inhabitants to survivors did not go smoothly. The UNRAA director for the European theater reported in an official complaint: "Despite explicit instructions … the Germans moved out their furniture and fixtures, removing even electric fixtures, ovens, etc. … The movement of furniture was carried out under the noses of the German civil police. In fact, they literally turned their backs when they saw the furniture being moved. The action of the police was nothing less than a conspiracy to defeat the order of evacuation given by the Military Government."[3]

As Szlama and Chaja had heard, Zeilsheim's living quarters did exceed conditions in most of the other DP camps, though hardly deluxe. They were severely overcrowded, with three families living in a two-room unit. Nevertheless, the quarters were luxurious compared to other camps.[4] Some DP camps were set up in former concentration camps. In the Babenhausen DP camp, the survivors' "flats" were the horse stalls of the former Third Reich cavalry. Survivors were so repulsed they did not want to leave the trains that brought them there. In another DP camp, Türkheim, 450 Jews lived behind a fence that was still electrified.[5]

Once settled, the Jews of Zeilsheim quickly got down to the business of recreating purposeful lives. They established key community institutions: hospitals, cooking facilities, arrangements for clothing distribution, educational and vocational training, and cultural and religious activities. They even began printing a Yiddish newspaper, *Untervegs (On the Move)*.[6]

A subcommittee that handled culture and welfare affairs tried to combat feelings of despair among the population by organizing events and programs that helped bring the community together and focus on the future, particularly preparation for immigration. According to Judah Nadich, the US Army's senior Jewish chaplain in Europe, 90 percent of DPs in Zeilsheim stated their intention to immigrate to Palestine. After the Holocaust, Zionism filled a symbolic need that had arisen for the Jewish people in the wake of tragedy, even among those who did not make the Zionist dream their personal reality. In the words of one survivor who intended to live in Montevideo, Uruguay, but responded to a survey that he would make Aliyah (Hebrew word for immigration to Israel), "I may be able to live in Uruguay, but the Jews ... the Jews must live in Israel."[7]

The leadership in Zeilsheim was dominated by stateless Eastern European Zionists. They even established two kibbutzim (collective communities in Israel based on agriculture), both of which operated on a communal basis and stressed training for life in the new land. One focused on agricultural training, the other on vocational training. Even DPs who didn't have plans to immigrate to Palestine, as the region was called (Israel wouldn't become a state until 1948), supported Zionism due to their fervent belief that a Jewish homeland was necessary. Large numbers of students crowded the camp's English-language classes, indicative of the many DPs who wished to settle in the United States.[8]

One of the highlights of the strongly Zionist-leaning Zeilsheim was David Ben-Gurion's visit in October 1945. He was like a god to Zeilsheim's survivors. One DP who witnessed his visit said, "I don't think a visit by President Truman could cause as much excitement."[9]

Szlama, like most of Plonsk's Jewish youth, had belonged to a Zionist group. Naturally, when he and Chaja spoke of where they hoped to settle from Zeilsheim, he chose Palestine. He had always fantasized about living there, though he never would have left his extended family to do so. But now, Aliyah was in reach.

Chaja flatly refused when Szlama brought up how it would be to live there, in a Jewish homeland. "Palestine is a land of conflict! And I've had enough of war." She sat back in the chair in the quiet living room. It was the only time they were alone, when the others went to visit their families. "I want to have children someday," she said wistfully, choking back tears. "And I don't want them to grow up only to die in a war."

Szlama was quiet. He couldn't argue with that, even though it was hard to let go of his dream. "What about France?"

"I don't know anyone who has lived there," Chaja said.

"Mishke has relatives there. He said the quality of life is good, though we can't make as much money there as we can in the United States."

For whatever reason, the couple rejected France. When Szlama broached Palestine one last time, Chaja told him in no uncertain terms, "If you go to Palestine, you are going alone. I'm not going."

Her statement struck at Szlama's greatest vulnerability. Chaja feared once again living in a war zone, but Szlama was terrified of being alone, so it was decided. When the time came, they would immigrate to the United States.

THIRTY-FOUR

Having chosen to immigrate to the United States, where Chaja had an aunt living in the Bronx who could sponsor them, the couple got down to the business of living, marrying in a religious ceremony on December 11, 1945. Surah did not attend the wedding because she and Chaja had had an argument.

Liberation hadn't forged a stronger bond between the two cousins. In fact, survivors often had petty spats with even the closest of cosurvivor friends. They would fail to resolve their issues for years and then forget about them and resume their relationships, only to repeat the pattern. Relationships among survivors were often fraught with difficulties. They were psychologically damaged people whose interpersonal communication skills were sorely lacking. Most of them never received counseling, and they took their angst out on one another because their social circles often revolved primarily around other survivors.

After their wedding, Szlama and Chaja tried to start a family, but Chaja didn't conceive. This was hardly a surprise, as Szlama had only one testicle. It was surely a subject of anguish for them that they might never have a family. Elsewhere in Zeilsheim, newly married couples were wasting no time in getting pregnant, eager to rebuild what had been lost and to have children for whom they could name their deceased loved ones, per Jewish law.

With no children to care for, Chaja would later recall her two years as a young married woman in Zeilsheim as the most carefree of her life. She was a true lady of leisure, passing her time gossiping with her new friends and enjoying every minute. But she knew it wouldn't last. Eventually, she and Szlama would emigrate and start from scratch in a new country with strange ways and a foreign language. Moreover, Szlama would have to make an honest living, and she would be right there, working alongside him.

Szlama quickly immersed himself in the ways of the black market. Having received his undergraduate degree in smuggling, negotiating, trading, and selling at Auschwitz, he was ready to get an advanced degree in black marketeering. He was a quick student, soon making money hand over fist. Business was even better in Zeilsheim than in Berlin, and before long, he and Chaja rented an apartment independent of the DP camp system. They even employed a German maid, although the only food Chaja would let her prepare was hard-boiled eggs, fearing she might poison their food.

It didn't take long for Szlama to establish himself as a leading black marketeer, trading chocolate, cigarettes, and alcohol with the German prostitutes who serviced the US soldiers. It was a perfect triangle. The American soldiers were paid in scrip notes, a currency that only had value in the army's PX (post exchange) where consumer goods were sold. The soldiers paid the German ladies who serviced them in these scrips and sometimes in cash. The prostitutes couldn't redeem the scrip. But Szlama could supply them with the various consumer goods they wanted in exchange for cash and their worthless scrips. Then he spent his earnings on more consumer goods, or sold the scrips to the soldiers at a slightly reduced rate.

Another moneymaking scheme of Szlama's was to hold on to his dollars, rubles, marks, pounds, or gold coins until their value dropped, and then flood the market with a specific currency to make people scared that it was becoming worthless, making its value plummet even further. Then he'd buy the currency back at half the price. Szlama became a well-known dealer, earning the moniker Shlomo Kurnik (Sam the Chicken Dealer) and accruing partners, including his cousin, Meyer Fuks. Szlama was the money handler, waiting in town for distributions, dressed in the shabby clothes of a pauper so as not to arouse suspicion. In fact, he looked so poor that the out-of-towners who came to do business with him passed him by and ended up at his house, asking where he was. Chaja would say, "That was him on the corner."

They'd reply, "That was him? The way he was dressed, I didn't think he was worth a groschen!" (Polish penny).

Since the Jewish police considered black market activity a serious offense and had no qualms with locking up guilty fellow Jews, Szlama was incarcerated several times. Fortunately, Chaja knew whom to pay off, and her husband never spent a night in jail. Szlama had met his match in Chaja, but she was embarrassed by the negative attention her husband's confinements were receiving, even though she enjoyed the benefits of his illegal dealings. In other words, she wasn't sorry he was involved in the black market. She was just mad when he got caught.

One day, Szlama was walking in town and came face-to-face with a German man whom he recognized. The German stood still, a look of obvious astonishment on his face. Then the two men spontaneously embraced in a bear hug. It was the guard who'd "looked the other way" when Szlama escaped in April 1945.

Now the German looked considerably older. Not all Germans soldiers deserved the fate that the Third Reich had dealt them. This man had been forced by the Nazis to serve in the desperate final months of the war. Szlama was delighted to be given the opportunity to properly thank him for saving his life, and the two men rejoiced in each other's survival.

There were light moments too. While hitchhiking one day, Szlama and Chaja were standing at a bend in the road when a German driver shouted out from his car, "Bei dies kurve nicht glüklich!" (This curve is a dangerous, unlucky place to get picked up!) Szlama and Chaja immediately burst out laughing. The German word for curve happens to be identical to the Yiddish word for whore. They always had a chuckle when they remembered this.

Eventually things got too hot for Szlama to stay in Zeilsheim. The Americans had learned of one of his schemes: chocolate and cigarettes were being transported from a train to a truck headed to a Zeilsheim storage unit procured by Szlama. One of his trading partners, an American soldier, warned him. The intelligence officers had Szlama's name, and when he was caught, he was going to go to jail. It was time to leave Germany. There was no way he would be able to avoid prosecution this time. The Hebrew Immigrant Aid Society (HIAS) paid for the trip, no doubt happy to assist in getting a problem refugee and his wife out of the country.

On September 22, 1947, Chaja and Szlama boarded the USS *Marine Flasher* in Bremerhaven (Bremen), Germany. The *Marine Flasher* was famous for being the first ship to bring the Jewish refugees to the United States, on May 10, 1946.

Szlama was carrying $10,000 in the hollowed-out heel of his shoe. Surah's husband, Hymie Pass, was a shoemaker. He made shoes with fake soles and fake heels to store valuables. You couldn't walk in the shoes, but they could hold a lot of currency. If you were to look in Sam and Helen's suitcases, you would see a lot of shoes and little else. For this journey, Szlama had gold coins and hundred-dollar bills stowed in the shoes.

Chaja vomited from seasickness throughout the entire voyage. Ten days later when the ship docked in New York, the couple disembarked as the newly minted Sam and Helen Bagel.

THIRTY-FIVE

As the *Marine Flasher* sailed into New York Harbor, Sam and Helen stood on the deck with the other passengers, taking in the view of the Statue of Liberty. Helen couldn't wait to get off the boat. Even after ten days, she was still nauseous.

On Ellis Island, as they were being processed for entry into the United States, an official patted Sam on the back. The unexpected gesture translated to, "You'll be all right." Neither Sam nor Helen spoke a word of English; the contact with the American was a welcome reassurance.

The first thing they needed to do was find their sponsor, Helen's aunt, Esther Abromovitz. She was Helen's mother's sister, who had offered to bring Rachma over before the war.

The only address they had for her was Hudson Street, New York, but there were multiple Hudson Streets in the city, since each of the five boroughs often had identical street names. Finally, the Bagels located the correct home in the Bronx.

They were crushed to learn that the aunt had died between her sponsorship and their arrival. Even though Helen's family had been sending this aunt and uncle money during the Depression, where their plight was worse than in Poland, the uncle greeted them very coldly, fearing they wanted financial assistance from him.

To the couple who sorely needed an English-speaking liaison and a sympathetic family member to help them begin their new lives, it was a terrible blow. It was not lost on Sam or Helen how the uncle's reaction to their appearance wasn't that different from that of Helen's Polish neighbor when she returned to Zakroczym for her family's belongings. They left immediately and never saw him again.

With the help of the Hebrew Immigrant Aid Society, they secured an apartment in Brooklyn where there were many Yiddish-speaking real estate agents. They quickly found employment with Howard Clothes, Inc., a men's clothing business that had opened in 1924 and was owned by Jews. The company had a massive factory in Brooklyn in the area that is now known as Dumbo, for Down Under the Manhattan Bridge Overpass. Sam, who had worked as a tailor, sewed cuffs on pants. Helen worked attaching buttons. They were paid based on the volume of their work. The other employees became resentful because they were good at what they did and made more money than most of their colleagues.

One day, Helen came home to find Sam crying at the kitchen table. In front of him was a piece of paper in which he'd written the names in Yiddish of each of his brothers. Beside every name was a sketch of a flower. Sam often drew flowers, though he wasn't a great artist. To him, the flowers were a symbol of life, and drawing the flowers was a way to rekindle his brothers' spirits

Helen said, "Let's get out of here. Let's take a walk, go to the deli." She gently took the pencil from his hand and pulled him to his feet.

It was cold outside, and the fresh air reinvigorated him somewhat, but he was wracked with survivors' guilt. Why had he lived when his brothers had not?

Only Helen could empathize with him. She understood him completely, and she was strong. He thanked God, in whom he still believed, for bringing her into his life.

Sam and Helen had plenty of money, but being unable to speak English was a huge obstacle for them. Helen was frustrated when she asked for *zalt* and the shopkeeper couldn't understand that she needed salt. Sam misinterpreted the word *sandwich* for *son of a bitch*, a term he had undoubtedly picked up on the job. As tired as they were after working long days in the factory, Sam and Helen quickly realized they had to enroll in night school to learn English if they wanted to better their circumstances. Helen, who had been a star pupil back in Poland, was the quicker learner of the two. But Sam picked up cultural references. He learned that baseball was important in America; the Yankees were important to New Yorkers.

By February 1948, Sam had enough confidence in himself to tell Helen, "I'm not working for Howard Clothing for the rest of my life."

It was time to go back to what he knew best. He took a bus to Connecticut in search of a chicken farm to buy. Helen had wanted to accompany him, but a bus ticket was too expensive, now that they were saving for their future. The cost of her ticket would indeed have been a waste of money because Connecticut didn't pan out.

Next, Sam looked in southern New Jersey. Survivor friends thought he was crazy to look there. It was in the middle of nowhere, they told him. But being in the boondocks was affordable. Sam rented his first farm in Vineland, New Jersey, with enough land for four thousand birds. He'd been in the United States for less than six months.

THIRTY-SIX

Vineland already had Holocaust survivors starting new lives as chicken and egg farmers when Sam and Helen arrived. The town had a vibrant Jewish community, making it an advantageous place to start a business. The Jewish farmers spoke Yiddish, so Sam's weak, newly acquired English skills didn't inhibit his shrewd business sense. A Yiddish-speaking attorney named Sam Shapiro took a liking to him and was instrumental in helping him get a driver's license and a certificate of occupancy for the home on the rental property. Shapiro's wife was also an attorney, albeit a nonpracticing one. The Bagels and the Shapiros formed a real friendship and socialized together. Sam and Helen joined the synagogue in Vineland and made other friends there as well.

Next, Sam used part of his savings to buy a used pickup truck. The novelty of driving never wore off for him; he loved it. He sold his farm-fresh eggs at local markets and in Brooklyn for retail prices. In Brooklyn, once all his inventory was sold, he would refill his truck with fresh vegetables and fruit and bring them home for Helen to prepare.

Egg farming had become a booming industry in the 1940s. The US military had developed the first approved influenza vaccine, in which hens' eggs were used to grow the virus, and all soldiers were inoculated against the disease.[1] After World War II, vaccinations and vaccination research kept the demand for eggs high. (By 1950, the Korean War added to the demand for eggs, driving prices further up, as powdered eggs were a staple sent to the soldiers.)

These were wonderful times for the young couple. They had friends and an active social life meeting at people's houses to play games and cards. They grew plump from filling up on such treats as hot chocolate and scones filled to bursting with blueberries and sugar; South Jersey was a leading producer of blueberries. They also attended Communist meetings in this pre-McCarthyism time. Sam had a true interest; Helen went to socialize. Despite his Communist sympathies, Sam joined Helen in her enthusiasm for the United States as a country.

Business was so good that Sam and Helen left the Vineland farm after a year and rented a larger, six-thousand-bird farm in Dorothy, New Jersey, where they were among other Holocaust survivors who helped found a synagogue.

For Helen, the synagogue was a symbol of tradition rather than belief. Throughout the rest of her life, she would never be involved in the temple from a religious perspective. She had never even learned to read Hebrew, as Jewish girls hadn't received a Hebrew education but a cultural one back in Poland. But she could make a good hamantaschen, the three-pointed pastry eaten on Purim, and a perfectly braided challah for Shabbat. She knew all the holidays and their meanings. She even kept me out of school on Shavuos, a Jewish holiday commemorating the wheat harvest as well as Moses receiving the Torah from God—not nearly as auspicious as the High Holidays of Rosh Hashanah (Jewish New Year) and Yom Kippur (Day of Atonement). The only service that ever resonated with Helen was Yizkor, the memorial service recited four times a year for deceased parents and other relatives.

Religion was a completely different experience for Sam. Despite all he had endured, he still believed in God. When he prayed, he was in a near-meditative state. He wasn't a philosophical man. He never dwelled on existential questions such as, "Who am I?" or "What am

I?" Sam had his own belief system that didn't fit neatly into any box. He thought of himself as a Socialist, when in fact, he was a capitalist. He thought people should share what they had equally; day care should be available for everyone; the rich should share with the poor; all people are equal. But paradoxically, he hired people whom he sometimes ripped off, and, at times, he cheated on the weight of the chickens he bought. His belief system was rich, but he didn't practice it. He preached the game of equality but practiced the game of exploitation.

With Helen's assistance, they were making close to $6,000 a year, though they didn't have much time to spend their earnings; they worked 365 days a year. Business grew so quickly that they again needed a bigger farm a year later in 1950, moving to Estell Manor, also in South Jersey. The newest farm had the capacity for eight thousand chickens.

There were weekends when Sam would bring Helen's cousin Surah (now Sarah), her husband, Hymie, and their baby daughter, Ruthy, with him from Brooklyn to spend a week or two. Sometimes Sarah and the baby came alone. Hymie had a shoemaker shop, but he wasn't making nearly as much as Sam's $6,000 yearly haul. Still, Sarah put away two dollars every week, no matter how much money came in. Helen subsidized Sarah's savings. The two women were on friendly terms during this period; there was a lot of love between them. (It was not to last. Once their children grew older, they got into subtle competition with each other over their children's successes.)

The year 1951 brought a change. The couple left South Jersey for Englishtown, in the central part of New Jersey. Sam was ready to diversify by adding chicken dealing to his egg-selling business. It was a shrewd move. Leghorn chickens, the breed prevalent on Jersey farms, start laying eggs at eighteen weeks. As the chickens age, the eggs get bigger until they become jumbo size by eighteen months. Younger chickens typically lay two eggs every three days, and even more if they are being treated with antibiotics. But the older, jumbo-laying chickens only yield one egg every three days, and jumbo eggs have thinner shells that break more easily. It is unprofitable to keep chickens after two years, but by then, they are nice and fat (though too fat for use as broilers and fryers) and make wonderful soup.

In 1951, there were a few major slaughterhouses in the Lakewood area, in central Jersey. Sam wisely developed his business, while living in Englishtown, by buying old leghorns from farmers in the area whose inventory ranged anywhere from 2,500 to 25,000 birds and delivering them to a slaughterhouse belonging to a man named Sam Zuck. Once again, a wealthy, successful man took an interest in Sam and Helen, as the Shapiros had. The Zucks became personal friends of the Bagels, speaking Yiddish with them on occasion and inviting them to their beautiful Lakewood home for dinners. It was a symbiotic business relationship: Sam sold the old leghorns to Zuck for slaughter, and Zuck sold them at a higher price to Campbell's Soup in nearby Camden, New Jersey.

Every week, Sam would crisscross the central region of the state, from Hightstown to Flemington, from Somerville to Farmingdale, collecting old leghorns from farmers who needed to replace them with young, profit-making ones. He had two trucks by this time, which read, *If You Have Chickens for Sale, Call Bagel Hightstown8-2156*, with enough room to transport a total of fifteen hundred birds a day. With his trucks at full capacity, paying five cents per pound, he'd sell them to the slaughterhouse for eight cents per pound, making a profit of $150 a day. Even after paying overhead expenses, such as his helper's salary and gas, he was making more money than a teacher. Helen was working at a knife factory at the time, further augmenting their earnings.

The business became too large for Sam to manage alone, so he took on a partner named Willie, who moved in with them. Unfortunately, it was not a good move; Willie gave them a lot of problems, of which Sam and Helen never went into specifics, simply referring to the partnership as a dark period.

The year 1952 brought yet another move and a break with Willie, this time to a small town near Roosevelt called Elys Corner. A five-thousand-hen egg farm run by Helen, it was to be the last rental property for the couple. With Willie excised, Sam still needed a new partner for the chicken-dealing side of the business. This time he turned to family, partnering with his first cousin Meyer Fox, brother of Schlomo Fuks. Like Sam, Meyer had been married before the war and lost a wife and two sons in the gas chambers.

The two trucks were painted BAGEL & FOX on the sides. At first, the partnership was a success. Sam was happy to again have someone share the work, plus his inability to read or write in English was a detriment. Meyer had mastered the language perfectly by this time. But the idyll was not to last. Meyer had married a mentally ill Jewish-American woman named Rose who treated him terribly. She once had him arrested while he was in temple, claiming that he'd beaten her up. Meyer often came to Sam and Helen for comfort during his difficulties with his wife, which was easy to do since the two couples lived together in the rental house.

The Bagels were also the recipients of Rose's vitriol. When they were going for citizenship papers in 1952, she sent a letter to the state claiming that Helen was a Communist and a prostitute.

Despite Rose's interference, Sam and Helen went to the oral citizenship test. Sam and Helen felt it was important to be American citizens. They were living in America, doing business in America, and they had no plan to leave. But the high numbers of immigrants prior to the 1950s had forced changes in US immigration law. The Immigration and Naturalization Act of 1952 required a demonstration of understanding the English language as well as history. And Sam couldn't speak English well.

On the day of the test, Sam and Helen arrived at the immigration office. Seated on hard wooden benches, they anxiously awaited Sam's turn in a stuffy, somewhat crowded waiting room.

When his name was called, Sam Bagel approached the immigration officer.

"How are you?" the officer asked.

"Fine," Sam managed. Their friends had told them this was all part of the test. These beginning parts were easy for Sam. He knew conversational English like this, but he spoke broken English. If they had to leave America, they were going to go to Israel.

After a while, the test had more difficult questions about US history.

"What was the name of the war between the North and the South?"

Sam started to sweat, and he moved to his collar and began to loosen it. "Uh ..."

Suddenly, a voice called out clearly, "The Civil War."

Helen. Sam waited a beat, perhaps thinking that doing so would make it seem more like he knew the answer on his own.

"The Civil War," Sam said.

"Why does the flag have thirteen stripes?"

"There were thirteen colonies," shouted Helen.

"There were thirteen colonies," said Sam, again after a pause, his thick accent still present even though he did his best to mimic Helen's inflection.

She did this whenever he was stuck on a question. It wasn't so much that he didn't know the answers. He just didn't know how to phrase them in English. After this day, Sam and Helen became Americans.

The year 1953 was even more momentous for them. After years of renting farms, they became landowners when they bought ten acres in Hightstown, New Jersey, for $5,000, spending an additional $15,000 for the construction of a three-bedroom, one-bath ranch house on the property. It was time to settle down.

Helen had an insatiable desire for strawberries, and Sam would go into Brooklyn to get them for her. It wasn't long before Helen discovered she was finally expecting a baby. Her doctor was a family practitioner who told her that she would likely need a cesarean section. Back in Poland, many women had died from C-sections, so true to her pragmatic nature, Helen went to the bakery when her labor pains began and bought three loaves of bread, telling the baker of her coming demise.

The baker answered, "If you think you're going to die, why do you need so much bread?"

She responded, "Well, my husband still needs to eat!"

On October 28, 1953, more than eight years after my parents' liberation, I arrived by caesarean at the Paul Kimball Hospital in Lakewood, New Jersey, weighing a hefty nine pounds, eight ounces. The C-section had indeed been necessary. My parents named me Jerry, after the two grandfathers I would never meet: Yosef and Yossel.

My birth was proof that Sam could procreate. But even more significant, Sam had brought forth a new Jewish life to make up for his lost daughter. On a familial level, as the only surviving children from each of their families, Helen and Sam had issued forth a child to carry on their lineages. Having a child was a triumph.

Rose Fox's constant interference was reason enough for Sam to cut ties with Meyer. Then, a full-time employee named Joe Matuczescki told Sam that Meyer had been stupid enough to confess to him that he'd been lying about how much money he was receiving from the slaughterhouse. It was the final straw. Sam confronted Meyer about the embezzlement and said he was dissolving their partnership. An indignant Meyer sued. Sam countersued, and a contentious legal battle followed into 1953. In the courtroom, Helen and Sam were almost called for contempt because they got so upset with Meyer's lies that they couldn't keep from screaming out.

THIRTY-SEVEN

In July 1954, construction on the house was complete, and we moved into 313 Disbrow Hill Road, leaving the Foxes behind in the rental in Ely's Corner.

The new house had its own septic system and well, with a pump that never provided excessive water pressure to the shower; the water took a long time to heat up. To Sam and Helen, it was perfection. Joining us in the home, though in the basement, was Joe Matuczeski, whom my parents called Joe Bum, due to his habit of imbibing two pints of muscatel every night (and four pints on the weekends).

Sam first met Joe a month before I was born when he was sent from an employment agency to assist with the poultry business. Joe was a loner from the coal mining town of Wilkes-Barre in northeast Pennsylvania. He had come from a Polish family who had suffered so much during the Depression that they had *returned* to Poland for three years before retracing their steps back to Wilkes-Barre.

Joe was the black sheep of his family and never married. He served in an army unit that had invaded North Africa and Sicily during World War II, rising to the rank of sergeant. He had loved Sicily for its vineyards and the wine that came from them. After his honorable discharge at the end of the war, he reenlisted and was stationed for three years in Japan. His years in the service were the highlight of his life. Five years later, he was living with us, smoking two packs of cigarettes a day, and getting drunk in the basement after dinner, which he more than occasionally ate with us, speaking Polish. Joe, whom I thought of as an uncle figure, would live with our family for the rest of his life. He died in 1976 of metastatic lung cancer.

There were three houses across the street from us, all owned by various members of the Estenes family, Hungarian Catholics who grew fruits and vegetables on their combined sixty acres. Directly across lived Henry and Beatrice Estenes, née Solomon. Beatrice had converted from Judaism and attended church every Sunday. It was like a thumb in Sam's eye after what he had suffered in the name of Judaism. He told me later, "If I'd have known I was moving across the street from a *geshmata* (Yiddish word for rag, with multiple connotations, such as 'turn to rag,' for a person who had converted from Judaism to Christianity), I wouldn't have bought that property."

Life fell into a rhythm after my birth, as my parents were finally settled into the home where they would live for more than fifty years. There was not yet a working farm on the property, so Helen could devote all her time to being a wife and mother. Reminiscent of the brief period of leisure she had experienced in Zeilsheim, she spent her days caring for me, socializing with her mostly survivor friends, and cooking all her Eastern European delicacies. Every Shabbat dinner included matzah ball soup flavored brightly with dill from her garden, homemade gefilte fish, and perfectly roasted chicken with shiny honey-brown skin.

Helen's garden was a source of pride, measuring one hundred by four hundred feet. From it came rhubarb, strawberries, blackberries, beets, carrots, various herbs, tomatoes, zucchini, eggplant, scallions, peppers, brussels sprouts, okra, lima beans, string beans, lettuce, radishes, and cucumbers, from which she made her own pickles. She even produced her own farmer's cheese.

Sam, having had two business partnerships go sour, was not going to allow himself to be burned for a third time. Joe Bum became his right-hand man, but the business was never going to be split again. It rested squarely on his shoulders now. Every morning he rose at five o'clock, breakfasting on coffee, coffee cake, and grapefruit juice. From Mondays through Thursdays, he drove to Airport Road in Hightstown where there was an African American shanty town and a daily supply of labor. Sam and Joe and whoever was working for them that day would then gather chickens and deliver them to Zuck's slaughterhouse. It was a very dirty job.

The chickens had free reign in the coops, with manure and straw encrusting the ground. The men had to chase the chickens into the corner of the coop, using a screen to try to contain them, and then gather them up by their legs, three chickens in each hand, while the chickens pecked and scratched at them. Then the birds were carried to another worker who would put them into crates. The workday usually ended between three and four in the afternoon. For this, Sam's workers were paid a daily wage of five dollars.

On Fridays, Sam visited the farmers he did business with to confirm pickup dates for the coming week. He also visited new farmers to drum up business. Since he had so many business relationships, and the farmers had periods of time when their flocks weren't old enough for slaughter, Sam sometimes went months without seeing some of them.

Meyer knew this and attempted to recruit business for himself by telling these farmers that Sam had died. It only bought him so much time before Sam inevitably called on the farmers, who, shocked, said, "Sam! We thought you were dead!" Meyer lost complete credibility, and that was the end of his chicken-dealing days.

THIRTY-EIGHT

The next four years were filled with hard work but also deep satisfaction for Sam. He recalled, "I had heard there was gold in the streets in America, and for me it was true." All he had to do was hustle. He loved being a businessman; he loved having employees; he loved being successful; he loved to drive his trucks; he loved his freedom—this life he'd built within ten years of liberation.

Equally, he found joy in his personal life; he deeply loved his wife and son. His faith was stoked at the First Hebrew Farmers Association of Perrineville Synagogue, established by the Jewish farmers of the area in 1907. He felt comfortable and safe among his fellow congregants and donated eighteen dollars (the number symbolizing life) every Shabbat. On Sundays, he rested. If he had any posttraumatic stress (PTSD) from his past, there were never any outward signs of it.

But the traumas of the past hadn't left Sam and Helen completely unscathed. They both had chips on their shoulders and suppressed self-esteem, which contributed to them finding imperfections in others that boosted their feelings of self-worth. They were also a source of curiosity to some of their American-born Jewish neighbors, who wanted to know about the Holocaust. Others, they felt, simply looked down on them because of their different customs and thick accents.

In 1956, Helen became pregnant again, but the joy my parents felt was not to last. Helen gave birth to a full-term baby boy in August who lived for only a few hours. It was a devastating blow to the couple who had already lost so much. "Baby Boy Bagel" was buried in the town's Jewish cemetery. Unlike the previous losses they had suffered, this one had a resting place and a headstone that they could visit. (When I was ten, my mother told me I was the reason my baby brother had died; I'd had a fight with my friend Benny Rheinholz, and Benny had taken his anger out on my nine-months-pregnant mother by punching her in the stomach. She claimed that she leaked fluid after that, and that was why the baby didn't live.)

My parents put the baby's death in the mental space reserved for such tragedies and soldiered on, throwing themselves in readying their ten acres for the addition of a true farm. A large chicken coop was built on the property in 1958, adding to Helen's responsibilities, as Sam was still chicken dealing. Monday through Thursday, she collected a daily average of twelve thousand eggs, which were then graded by Sam when he came home in the afternoon.

One day, Sam and Helen visited a new meat shop in town. When they got to the counter, the butcher looked visibly shocked.

"Were you in Janina?" he asked Sam.

"Yes," Sam said. "Who are you?"

The butcher was David Yeger, the newly arrived Janina prisoner who had seen Szlama and had never forgotten his face. That was the only time David and Sam ever talked about the war; it was too painful for them to discuss, even though the two formed a friendship that day that lasted the rest of Sam's life.

In the spring of 1959, my mother learned she was expecting another baby. After an uneventful pregnancy, my brother Herbert was born on February 9, 1960, weighing almost eight and a half pounds. Herbie was named for Cheel, my father's oldest brother. Our family was now complete.

If anyone had told Helen while she was in Birkenau that she was going to survive, and not only that, have a loving husband, two sons, and a thriving business, she would have never believed it.

Sam, however, probably would have. His optimism to live *another day* had helped to pull him through where others gave up. He had been an active participant in his survival, whereas Helen *did* give up, when she refused to work for six weeks after her sister's death. But her strong body didn't fail her, and luck was with her when those who stood beside her at appel were snatched for the gas chambers while she was spared. The Holocaust was something that happened to her. She never participated in her survival.

THIRTY-NINE

By all outward appearances, we were no different from any of the other solidly middle-class families in the area. My parents worked hard and took great satisfaction in their success; they were proud that they owned their own business and didn't have to answer to anyone else. Herbie and I thrived growing up on the farm, where there was plenty of room to play, plenty of food to eat, a temple that supplied us with a social life, and a swim club to cool off in during the summers.

After years of riding around in Dad's pickup truck, my parents purchased their first car, a mustard-gold 1959 Pontiac Star Chief. It was an American symbol of success, followed by another: the addition of a breezeway and a two-car garage to our home. In 1963, my parents expanded the farm by doubling the amount of square feet they utilized, replacing the coop with cages, allowing them to double their chicken/egg inventory. Two years later, they expanded again. My mother was still running the farm, packing an average of seven thousand dozen eggs a week, while my dad still dealt in leghorns.

Life at home had a comforting, predictable rhythm. We came together as a family at the dinner table. Food was one thing my parents didn't scrimp on. My mom would order a quarter of a cow, 150 pounds of meat, from a butcher in Lakewood who cut up our portion and delivered it to our freezer. It would last a year.

Indeed, we ate so well that my mother contracted type 2 diabetes in 1963. (In true Helen fashion, she blamed me for it, berating me, "You were such a fat baby you gave me diabetes," when in fact, the opposite was true. I was so fat *because* she had suffered from gestational diabetes, which contributed to her later diagnosis.)

Helen was one for extremes. Just as she thought she'd die giving birth to me, she assumed her diabetes would turn her into a cripple. With her customary determination, she whittled her weight down, cutting out treats such as ice cream and baked goods. She took her medicine and saw her doctor regularly.

The change in my mother's diet didn't alter our lives. Every evening, my father signaled the day's end by enjoying one shot of vodka. At six o'clock, we ate. A typical non-Sabbath meal consisted of steak cooked well done, accompanied by vegetables cooked well done, with Jell-O for dessert. After eating, like many American families, we'd go into the TV room (the third bedroom) to watch *The Three Stooges* and *Abbott and Costello*. On Sundays, we enjoyed *The Ed Sullivan Show* and *Bonanza*. Dad especially liked Mutual of Omaha's *Wild Kingdom* because he didn't have to understand English to enjoy it.

My parents worked every bit as hard in the summers, but at the day's end, we joined the mostly Jewish members of the Hilltop Swim Club to let off steam. Dad loved to swim and dive off the diving board. Mom couldn't swim and had no interest in learning, since she'd been raised on the story of her grandfather drowning in the Vistula River back in Poland.

Some of my best memories are from the nights my mom packed our dinner in a picnic hamper, which she did about twice a week, and us eating in the grass at the club. There were hardly any other members there at that hour, and it was so peaceful. My mom would make us wait after eating, lest we get a cramp and drown, and when the allotted time was up, we could return to the pool.

Another summer pastime for my parents was going to watch wrestling matches at the convention center in Asbury Park. Dad would drag Mom to the venue, but he couldn't make her go in. She preferred the movie theater across the street. When *Sound of Music* came out, she saw it three times she loved it so much. They both loved the park's swan boat ride and the fun house. They got a special kick out of the mirrors that made them look fat or small.

Aside from the swim club and the Perrineville Jewish Center, their social life revolved around the Bar Mitzvahs we attended, mostly in Brooklyn, of fellow survivors' children. Beginning in 1960, when the first of these offspring reached the age of thirteen, we went at least once a month to mammoth affairs that were in complete contrast to the sponge cake and wine repasts of Poland. For the survivors, the receptions they held were a chance to show to friends (most who had no extended family) how successful they'd become. Multiple-piece bands were hired; new dresses were purchased. My mom repainted her shoes to match every new gown she wore. (It was unheard of to wear the same dress to multiple affairs.)

My Bar Mitzvah, on November 5, 1966, was no exception. After completing my service, all in Hebrew except for my speech, we left for Brooklyn, where my parents hosted what I thought was a lavish reception in the evening. Looking back, it was just like all the others we had attended. Herbie became a Bar Mitzvah in 1973, and by then, in keeping with their pattern of upward mobility, my parents had more money to spend. Herbie's party was a little more sophisticated, catered in upscale Short Hills, New Jersey.

Nine months before my Bar Mitzvah, while I was knee-deep in preparations and my parents were planning the party, my father began to reminisce about his own ceremony many years before. He'd been attending his friends' affairs for six years, seen them paste too-big smiles on their faces and dance the hora with forced energy, as if to stamp out the memory of all the family members not in attendance. He began to think of the family he still had, namely Meyer Fox. Yes, Meyer had cheated him and sued him. Yes, Meyer's wife was a horrible woman. But Meyer was blood, someone who had known *all* the parts of him, not just the Americanized version. Meyer was the only person in the world who had known his first wife, Tovah, and his daughter. No one else, not even Helen, knew him so completely.

The realization was enough for Sam to vanquish his enmity toward Meyer completely. They had seen each other from time to time since ending their partnership, usually sitting outside under the trees on our farm, but that had been the extent of it. This time, my father reached out with an olive branch, and Meyer grabbed hold of it. The cousins began to socialize within a renewed bond.

When my Bar Mitzvah came around, the two cousins planned to dance together as they had done in Poland. But it was not to be. Meyer suffered a heart attack a week before my ceremony, though he did recover and attended Herbie's Bar Mitzvah seven years later.

The pattern of breaking off friendships and renewing them as if nothing had happened was a common practice of survivors, and my parents were no different. My mother and my aunt Sarah often went through periods of not speaking; my father and his friend Schmeel, a survivor who lived down the road, did as well. In fact, it was so common there was even a Yiddish word for it—*broyguss*, roughly translating to not speaking with someone because you are angry with them, only to rekindle the relationship a few years later. Why was this behavior so prevalent among survivors? Wouldn't one think that, with all they'd lost, they'd hold their close relationships especially dearly? Or was the difficulty in maintaining interpersonal relationships a symptom of the posttraumatic stress disorder (PTSD) from which they surely suffered?

My parents didn't dwell on their feelings, and they didn't reach out to others to unburden themselves either. They avoided conflict and just got on with it. If they had a problem with someone, they literally quit that person, often resuming the relationship later. They'd had enough conflict in their lives during the war; it was repugnant for them to engage in anything nasty when they now had a choice of whether to do so.

There were other signs of their past traumas too. My mother *never* left the house without putting food in her purse and at least forty dollars in her wallet, which was a lot of money to carry around in the 1960s. My father couldn't abide mediocre soup. Food was a different story, but he always said he'd rather have one spoonful of good soup than a bowl of bad soup, no doubt from the slop he'd been forced to imbibe for his survival. During the Yom Kippur holiday, when Jews were required to fast for a day, my mother would tell us, "You don't need to fast because I fasted for all of you."

When my parents attended funerals, where Jewish custom is for everyone in attendance to shovel a symbolic bit of dirt upon the coffin, my father would shovel much more dirt than was customary, as if he was attending to the burial needs of all those souls who hadn't been given proper burials.

My mother never cried at funerals, whereas my father cried like a baby at Meyer's funeral in 1974.

"Why are you crying? He cheated you all the time," I said.

He said, "I am again alone."

I answered, "You have me, Herbie, and Mom."

He just looked at me like I was crazy.

My whole life, my father never talked about the events of his life pertaining to his first family. In fact, I didn't learn of their existence until after my father's death. I thought I knew my parents' story.

I was not angry that he never told me; everyone deserves their own sanctity. The loss he kept from me and my brother was too much for him to share. It's even difficult for me to feel that I had a sister.

But again, Meyer had known them. In my father's eyes, the death of the last person on earth besides himself to have known Tovah and their daughter must have been like losing them all over again.

FORTY

In 1973, the year my dad turned sixty, he stopped chicken dealing. He and my mother continued raising chickens on their farm until 1978. Sam peddled eggs, and Helen took a part-time job as an egg packer on a nearby farm. Their income was supplemented by monthly $250 payments in reparations from the German government, with each of my parents having received a lump sum of between $12,000 and $15,000 in the 1960s.

I graduated from medical school in 1981 and began an internship in Miami, Florida. That year, my parents finally began to dip their toes into the idea of retirement, beginning the first of many happy years of spending three months every winter in a rented condo in Hallandale. They loved playing cards by the pool with friends (mostly survivors) and shopping. Herbie and I referred to their community as "Little Auschwitz."

In 1983, I married a Jewish Colombian woman of Ashkenazi (Eastern European) descent named Frida. My parents were delighted for two reasons: she wasn't a shiksa (they had told me if I ever married one, they'd kill themselves), and she spoke Yiddish. Two years later, my fellowship in dermatology completed, I started my own practice in East Windsor, New Jersey. I still can't explain why I chose to return home. Was it a shrewd business decision? Or subliminally, was the pull of my parents too strong? They'd lost their families. How could I settle permanently far away from them?

Herbie married a woman named Stacey in 1986, and the arrival of grandchildren followed. My son, Rick, was born later that year on August 4, 1986. His bris (circumcision ceremony) eight days later was one of the happiest days of my parents' lives. Three years later, Frida and I welcomed a daughter, Bridget. My mother dampened my dad's pleasure by insensitively commenting to him, "Such a nice thing to have a baby girl. You know, from this, Sam." My dad replied that he didn't want to talk about it, and to this day, I don't know the name of my half sister. (Perhaps my mother's comment betrayed an insecurity she carried about not being my father's first wife.) Their third grandchild arrived in 1990 when Herbie and Stacey had a daughter named Ilana.

In late May 1991, on the holiday of Shavuot, Dad's health began to deteriorate, and he was hospitalized with a heart attack. He was seventy-seven. After unsuccessful bypass surgery, my father passed away on July 18, 1991. Just before he died, he reflected on his life: "What did I live through?" They were his last words.

The sadness of Dad's passing was assuaged a bit when Herbie and Stacey welcomed a son the following July. They named him Sam.

Helen spent three more years in the house on Disbrow Hill Road before deciding it was too much for her. She settled contentedly into a retirement community in nearby Monroe, New Jersey. It was the right decision: two years later, in 1996, she suffered a minor stroke that required her to undergo carotid bypass surgery. She made a full recovery.

In November 2004, when my son, Rick, was a student at Duke University in North Carolina, Herbie, Bridget, and I went down to visit him and attend a Duke Blue Devils basketball game. Rick and Bridget hung out before the game and made plans to meet up with Herbie and me outside the venue.

On our way, Herbie suddenly appeared disoriented and collapsed midsentence. One minute we were talking, the next minute he was down. I attempted to give him CPR, as did other bystanders, but to no avail. My brother was pronounced dead at Duke Medical Center on November 21, 2004, of a myocardial infarction brought on by diabetes. He was only forty-four years old.

As devastating as Herbie's loss was to me and my children, I now had to tell my eighty-one-year-old, widowed mother, who had already suffered unimaginable loss, that her child had died.

I got to her house early in the morning, after having returned from North Carolina late the night before. Immediately, she knew something was wrong. "Why are you here so early?" she asked.

"Mom, I have some bad news. Herbie had a heart attack. He didn't make it."

Mom's face went slack and turned white.

"Hoybie died? Yetz ich vill nish meir lieben." (Now I don't want to live anymore.)

It was heartbreaking. I knew she meant it. The last time she had felt that way, she'd tried to commit suicide by refusing to work for six weeks in Auschwitz.

She was stoic at the funeral and didn't shed a tear. "I can't cry because I don't have any tears left," she told me. One week after we buried Herbie, Mom was admitted to the hospital with chest pains. Perhaps she would get her wish this time. But instead, she endured emergency bypass surgery and a full recovery. Her body simply wouldn't give out. She was still too strong.

Mom's demeanor changed for a time after we lost Herbie. She became depressed and removed, as one would expect. She told me that losing a child was more painful than the loss of her family in the Holocaust. She recalled how she had refused to move to Israel many years before because she hadn't wanted her children to risk their lives in a war-torn society. She'd moved to the States, and her child had died anyway.

Gradually, however, she came back. Her friends called regularly to check on her, and sometimes she attended the social activities in her community. She spent a lot of time doing things that made her happy, namely spending time with and babysitting my children. She and Bridget grew especially close.

In 2007, my mother suffered a serious stroke that weakened her left side. She couldn't drive anymore, and she needed a walker to get around. Living alone was no longer possible, so she moved in with my family. But she wasn't happy, even with her grandchildren around. She'd always been so strong and independent, and now she was compromised and living in another woman's home. Within a year, she asked if she could go into an assisted-living facility, and in 2008, we granted her that wish. It is now ten years later. My mother just celebrated her ninety-fifth birthday. She doesn't talk that much, and she's in a wheelchair, but Helen Bagel is still a force. Her strong body is not ready to quit.

EPILOGUE

As a medical doctor, I've thought about how Holocaust survivors like my parents may have exhibited posttraumatic stress disorder (PTSD). The vast majority were hardworking, successful individuals, who wanted more than anything else to make a better life for their themselves and—even more so—for their children. They didn't see therapists, and they weren't on psychiatric meds. They worked.

Once when I was about fifteen, sitting at the kitchen table, my dad asked me, "What's wrong?"

I said, "I'm bored."

He replied, "Do you have something to eat, a place to live? Is anyone trying to kill you? You are not bored!"

Writing this book has kept me in contact with my dad. I thank G-d my mom is still with us, and we can still make each other laugh. The fact that she can laugh after all she has gone through should connect us all to the spirit in the human soul.

ENDNOTES

Chapter 1

1   Shlomo Zemach, ed., *Memorial Book of Plonsk and Vicinity* (Tel-Aviv: 1963), 31.
2   www.kehilalinks.jewishgen.org/plonsk/history.
3   Bernard Reich and David H. Goldberg, *Historical Dictionary of Israel* (Scarecrow Press, 2008), 558.
4   David Ben-Gurion, *Memoirs* (World Publishing, 1970), 36.
5   www.jewishvirtuallibrary.org/david-ben-gurion.
6   Piotr S. Wandycz, "The Polish Question," in *The Treaty of Versailles: A Reassessment after 75 Years* (New York: Cambridge University Press, 1998), 313–36.
7   www.yadvashem.org/yv/en/exhibitions/communities/plonsk/politics.asp.

Chapter 2

1   S. Spector and G. Wigoder, eds., "Zakroczym," in *The Encyclopedia of Jewish Life before and during the Holocaust,* vol. 3 (New York: 2001), 1484.
2   www.polska.pl/tourism/urban-tourism/modlin/.
3   www.sztetl.org.pl/en/towns/z/418-zakroczym/99-history/138295-history-of-community.
4   www.zchor.org/zakroczym/zakroczym.htm.

Chapter 3

1   William L. Shirer, *The Rise and Fall of the Third Reich: A History of Nazi Germany* (Simon & Schuster, 1990), 281–302.
2   Joshua D. Zimmerman, *Contested Memories: Poles and Jews During the Holocaust and Its Aftermath* (Rutgers University Press, 2003), 19.
3   Eli Valley, *The Great Jewish Cities of Central and Eastern Europe: A Travel Guide Resource Book to Prague, Warsaw, Crakow, and Budapest* (Jason Aaronson, 1999), 164.
4   Emanuel Melzer, *No Way Out: The Politics of Polish Jewry, 1935–1939* (Cincinnati: Hebrew Union College Press, 1965), 90.
5   Abraham Brumberg, *New York Review of Books*, August 18, 1983.
6   Melzer, *No Way Out: The Politics of Polish Jewry, 1935–1939*, 91.
7   Roderick Stackelberg, *The Routledge Companion to Nazi Germany* (Routledge, 2007), 155–57.

Chapter 4

1   www.ushmm.org/wlc/en/article.php?ModuleId=10005469.
2   www.eurojewcong.org/communities/poland/.
3   Gerhard L. Weinberg, *The Foreign Policy of Hitler's Germany* (Humanity, 1995), 57–.
4   Richard J. Evans, *The Third Reich in Power* (Penguin, 2005), 674–76.
5   www.yadvashem.org/yv/en/holocaust/resource_center/faq.asp.
6   www.ushmm.org/outreach/en/article.php?ModuleId=10007698.
7   Stackelberg, *The Routledge Companion to Nazi Germany*, 14.
8   Evans, *The Third Reich in Power*, 580–86.
9   Ibid., 591.
10 www.history.com/topics/kristallnacht.
11 Ruth Gay, *The Jews of Germany: A Historical Portrait* (Yale, 1994), xiii.
12 Alexandra Garbarini, *Jewish Responses to Persecution: 1938–1940* (Documenting Life and Destruction: Holocaust Sources in Context, 2013), 3–4.
13 Evans, *The Third Reich in Power*, 703.
14 Ibid., 692–93.

Chapter 5

1 James S. Corum, "The Luftwaffe's Campaigns in Poland and the West 1939–1940: A Case Study of Handling Innovation in Wartime," *Security and Defense Quarterly* (2013): 168–69.

2 *TIME* Staff, "Grey Friday: *TIME* Reports on World War II Beginning," *TIME* XXXIV, no. 11 (September 11, 1939).

3 www.ushmm.org/learn/timeline-of-events/1939-1941/britain-and-france-declare-war.

4 www.yadvashem.org/yv/en/exhibitions/communities/plonsk/during_holocaust.asp.

5 Ibid.

6 Zemach, *Memorial Book of Plonsk and Vicinity*, 446–47.

7 Zemach, *Memorial Book of Plonsk and Vicinity*, 429–30.

8 www.yadvashem.org/yv/en/exhibitions/communities/plonsk/religious_life.asp.

9 www.yadvashem.org/yv/en/exhibitions/communities/plonsk/during_holocaust.asp.

10 Testimony of Joe Engel, https.//collections.ushmm.org/search/catalog/irn505519.

11 Jan T. Gross, *Revolution from Abroad: The Soviet Conquest of Poland's Western Ukraine and Western Belorussia* (Princeton: Princeton University Press, 2000), 17.

12 www.yadvashem.org/yv/en/exhibitions/communities/plonsk/during_holocaust.asp.

13 Ibid.

14 Gennady Estraikh, "The Missing Years: Yiddish Writers in Soviet Bialystok, 1939–41," *East European Jewish Affairs* 46, no. 2 (2016).

15 Sara Bender, *The Jews of Bialystok during World War II and the Holocaust* (Brandeis, 2008), 53.

16 Ibid.

17 Ibid.

18 www.yadvashem.org/yv/en/exhibitions/communities/plonsk/judenrat.asp.

19 Zemach, *Memorial Book of Plonsk and Vicinity*, 453.

20 www.yadvashem.org/yv/en/exhibitions/communities/plonsk/judenrat.asp.

21 www.ushmm.org/wlc/en/article.php?ModuleId=10005069.

22 www.ushmm.org/wlc/en/article.php?ModuleId=10005130.

23 www.yadvashem.org/yv/en/exhibitions/communities/plonsk/
    ghetto.asp.
24 www.yadvashem.org/yv/en/exhibitions/communities/plonsk/
    ghetto.asp.
25 Henry Ramek, as told to Eve Gordon-Ramek and Anne Grenn
    Saldinger, *My Will to Live* (Friesen Press, 2014), 39.
26 www.yadvashem.org/yv/en/exhibitions/communities/plonsk/
    ghetto.asp.

Chapter 6

1 S. Spector and G. Wigoder, eds., *The Encyclopedia of Jewish Life before
    and during the Holocaust*, vol. 3 (New York: 2001), 1484.
2 Shirer, *The Rise and Fall of the Third Reich: A History of Nazi Germany*,
    845–52.

Chapter 7

1 John A. Armstrong, "Collaborationism in World War II: The Integral
    Nationalist Variant in Eastern Europe," *Journal of Modern History* 40,
    no. 3 (September 1968): 409.
2 www.ushmm.org/wlc/en/article.php?ModuleId=10005421.
3 www.ushmm.org/wlc/en/article.php?ModuleId=10005130.
4 Richard Rhodes, *Masters of Death: The SS-Einsatzgruppen and the
    Invention of the Holocaust* (New York: Vintage, 2002), 168.
5 www.ushmm.org/wlc/en/article.php?ModuleId=10005477.
6 www.ushmm.org/outreach/en/article.php?ModuleId=10007714.
7 www.ushmm.org/wlc/en/article.php?ModuleId=10007183.
8 www.jewishvirtuallibrary.org/crematoria-and-gas-chambers-
    at-auschwitz-birkenau.
9 www.ushmm.org/wlc/en/article.php?ModuleId=10005477.
10 www.sztetl.org.pl/en/towns/p/595-plonsk/99-history/137855-history-
    of-community.
11 www.yadvashem.org/yv/en/exhibitions/communities/plonsk/ghetto_
    liquidation.asp.

Chapter 8

1   www.ushmm.org/wlc/en/article.php?ModuleId=10007259.
2   www.holocaustresearchproject.org/othercamps/auschwitzgas chambers.html.
3   Danuta Czech, *Auschwitz Chronicle* (New York: Henry Holt & Company, 1989), 146.
4   Ibid., 191.
5   Miklos Nyiszli, *Auschwitz: A Doctor's Eyewitness Account* (Arcade, 2011), 38–54.
6   www.holocaustresearchproject.org/othercamps/auschwitzgas chambers.html.
7   Ibid.
8   Czech, *Auschwitz Chronicle*, 546.
9   www.ushmm.org/wlc/en/article.php?ModuleId=10007904.
10 Yisrael Gutman and Michael Berenbaum, eds., *Anatomy of the Auschwitz Death Camp* (Indiana University, 1998), 250–55.
11 www.jewishvirtuallibrary.org/crematoria-and-gas-chambers-at-auschwitz-birkenau.
12 David Cymet, *History vs. Apologetics: The Holocaust, the Third Reich and the Catholic Church* (Lexington: 2012), 280.
13 Czech, *Auschwitz Chronicle*, 127–28.
14 www.jewishvirtuallibrary.org/crematoria-and-gas-chambers-at-auschwitz-birkenau.
15 Ibid.

Chapter 9

1   Zemach, *Memorial Book of Plonsk and Vicinity*, 482.
2   Rawson, *Auschwitz: The Nazi Solution: An Illustrated History and Guide* (Pen and Sword Military, 2015), chapter 7.
3   Seymour Mayer, *And Then the Nazis Came* (Xlibris, 2010), 67.

Chapter 10

1   www.yadvashem.org/yv/en/exhibitions/communities/plonsk/ghetto_liquidation.asp.
2   www.ushmm.org/wlc/en/article.php?ModuleId=10005445.

3   Gideon Greif, *We Wept Without Tears: Testimonies of the Jewish Sonderkommando from Auschwitz* (Yale University, 2014), 314.
4   www.yadvashem.org/yv/en/exhibitions/communities/plonsk/overview.asp.
5   Czech, *Auschwitz Chronicle*, 287–88.
6   Ibid.

Chapter 11

1   www.jewishvirtuallibrary.org/memoranda-to-himmler.
2   Robert Jay Lifton, *The Nazi Doctors: Medical Killing and the Psychology of Genocide* (Basic, 1988), 21.
3   Czech, *Auschwitz Chronicle*, 262–63.
4   Testimony of Morris Dach, www.vimeo.com/14967703.
5   Lifton, *The Nazi Doctors: Medical Killing and the Psychology of Genocide*, 283–86.
6   Ibid.
7   Ibid.
8   Ibid.
9   Czech, *Auschwitz Chronicle*, 294.
10   Lifton, *The Nazi Doctors: Medical Killing and the Psychology of Genocide*, 283–86.
11   Ibid.
12   Ibid.
13   Ibid.
14   Czech, *Auschwitz Chronicle*, 616.

Chapter 12

1   Czech, *Auschwitz: Nazi Death Camp. Auschwitz-Birkenau State Museum*, 97.
2   Primo Levi, *Survival in Auschwitz and the Reawakening: Two Memoirs* (New York: Summit Books, 1986), 82.
3   www.yadvashem.org/odot_pdf/Microsoft%20Word%20-%206474.pdf.

Chapter 15

1   www.auschwitz.org/en/history/the-ss-garrison/.
2   www.collections.ushmm.org/search/catalog/vha45132.

Chapter 16

1   www.ideajournal.com/articles.php?id=16.
2   Czech, *Auschwitz Chronicle*, 240, 650–51, 710.
3   Tzipora Silberstein, *Yad Vashem Archives* 03/5467 (May 21, 1989): 1–23.
4   Czech, *Auschwitz Chronicle*, 240, 650–51, 710.
5   www.nybooks.com/articles/1987/12/17/beyond-judgment/.

Chapter 17

1   www.sciencedirect.com/science/article/pii/S1553465006006613.
2   Hermann Langbein, *People in Auschwitz* (University of North Carolina, 2015), 403.
3   Ibid.
4   Ibid.
5   Ibid.

Chapter 18

1   Geoffrey P. Megargee, *The United States Holocaust Memorial Museum Encyclopedia of Camps and Ghettos, 1933–1945*, vol. 1 (Indiana University Press, 2009), 253–54.
2   Ibid., 254.
3   Ibid.
4   Peter Hayes, *Industry and Ideology: I. G. Farben in the Nazi Era* (Cambridge: 2001), 360.
5   Megargee, *The United States Holocaust Memorial Museum Encyclopedia of Camps and Ghettos, 1933–1945*, vol. 1, 254.
6   Ibid.
7   Ibid.
8   Ibid.

9   www.yadvashem.org/yv/en/exhibitions/bearing-witness/carbide-lamp.asp.
10 Author conversation with David Yeger, August 2016.

Chapter 19

1   Testimony of Morris Dach, www.vimeo.com/14967703.

Chapter 20

1   Richard G. Davis, *Bombing the European Axis Powers: A Historical Digest of the Combined Bomber Offensive 1939–1945* (Air University, 2006), 275–88.
2   www.airforcemag.com/MagazineArchive/Magazine%20 Documents/2015/August%202015/0815goering.pdf.
3   Roy M. Staney, *V - Weapons Hunt: Defeating German Secret Weapons* (Casemate, 2010), 275–88.
4   Author conversation with David Yeger, August 2016.
5   Langbein, *People in Auschwitz*, 261.
6   Ibid.
7   Author conversation with David Yeger, August 2016.
8   Shirer, *The Rise and Fall of the Third Reich: A History of Nazi Germany*, 1090–96.
9   Antony Beevor, *Ardennes 1944: The Battle of the Bulge* (Penguin, 2016), 351.
10 Michael J. Lyons, *World War II: A Short History* (Prentice Hall, 1994), 270.
11 Joshua D. Zimmerman, *The Polish Underground and the Jews, 1939–1945* (Cambridge: 2015), 411.

Chapter 21

1   Czech, *Auschwitz Chronicle*, 782–83.
2   Sara Nomberg-Przytyk, *Auschwitz: True Tales from a Grotesque Land* (University of North Carolina, 1986), 129.
3   Czech, *Auschwitz Chronicle*, 785.
4   Livia Szabo Krancberg, *Two Sisters: A Journey of Survival through Auschwitz* (Library of the Holocaust, 2016), 155.

5   www.holocaustresearchproject.org/othercamps/auschdeathmarch.
    html.
6   Kershaw, *The End: The Defiance and Destruction of Hitler's Germany,
    1944–1945*, 232.
7   www.ushmm.org/outreach/en/article.php?ModuleId=10007734.
8   *Death Marches*, video, Holocaust History Museum, Yad Vashem.
9   Author conversation with Sarah Pass, May 2017.
10 Ian Kershaw, *The End: The Defiance and Destruction of Hitler's
    Germany, 1944–1945*, 334.
11 Krancberg, *Two Sisters: A Journey of Survival through Auschwitz*,
    156–57.
12 Ibid., 158.
13 www.ushmm.org/outreach/en/article.php?ModuleId=10007734.
14 Rochelle G. Saidel, *The Jewish Women of Ravensbrück Concentration
    Camp* (University of Wisconsin, 2006), 135.

Chapter 22

1   Megargee, *The United States Holocaust Memorial Museum Encyclopedia
    of Camps and Ghettos, 1933–1945*, vol. 1, 253.
2   Ibid.
3   Filip Müller, *Eyewitness Auschwitz: Three Years in the Gas Chambers*
    (Ivan R. Dee, 1999), 165–66.
4   www.ushmm.org/learn/timeline-of-events/1942-1945/death-march-
    from-auschwitz.
5   William I. Hitchcock, *The Bitter Road to Freedom: A New History of
    the Liberation of Europe* (Simon and Schuster, 2008), 293.
6   www.auschwitz.org/en/history/evacuation/the-final-evacuation-
    and-liquidation-of-the-camp.
7   Daniel Goldhagen, *Hitler's Willing Executioners: Ordinary Germans
    and the Holocaust* (Knopf Doubleday, 2007), 588.
8   Megargee, *The United States Holocaust Memorial Museum Encyclopedia
    of Camps and Ghettos, 1933–1945*, vol. 1, 255.
9   www.ushmm.org/wlc/en/article.php?ModuleId=10005454.

Chapter 23

1 www.jewishvirtuallibrary.org/history-and-overview-of-ravensbr-uuml-ck.

2 Paul R. Bartrop, Michael Dickerman, eds., *The Holocaust: An Encyclopedia and Document Collection* (ABC-CLIO 2017), 479.

3 Saidel, *The Jewish Women of Ravensbrück Concentration Camp*, 30.

4 www.yadvashem.org/articles/interviews/solzbach.html.

5 Rena Kornreich Gelissen, *Rena's Promise: A Story of Sisters in Auschwitz* (Beacon, 1995), 252.

6 Louis Brandsdorfer, *The Bleeding Sky: My Mother's Journey through the Fire* (CreateSpace, 2012), 96.

7 Saidel, *The Jewish Women of Ravensbrück Concentration Camp*, 128.

8 Brandsdorfer, *The Bleeding Sky: My Mother's Journey through the Fire*, 96.

9 Ibid., 100.

10 Saidel, *The Jewish Women of Ravensbrück Concentration Camp*, 100.

11 Ibid., 124.

12 Megargee, *The United States Holocaust Memorial Museum Encyclopedia of Camps and Ghettos, 1933–1945*, vol. 1, 560–64.

13 www.jewishgen.org/ForgottenCamps/Witnesses/HornEng.html.

14 Blatman, *The Death Marches*, 131.

Chapter 24

1 www.yadvashem.org/articles/general/women-in-ravensbrueck.html.

2 Megargee, *The United States Holocaust Memorial Museum Encyclopedia of Camps and Ghettos, 1933–1945*, vol. 1, 216.

3 Krancberg, *Two Sisters: A Journey of Survival through Auschwitz*, 165.

4 Ibid., 165–66.

5 Jack Gaylord Morrison, *Ravensbrück: Everyday Life in a Women's Concentration Camp, 1939–45* (2000), 215–16.

6 Sarah Helm, *Ravensbrück: Life and Death in Hitler's Concentration Camp for Women* (Anchor, 2015), 557.

7 Saidel, *The Jewish Women of Ravensbrück Concentration Camp*, 133–34.

8 Rena Kornreich Gelissen, *Rena's Promise: A Story of Sisters in Auschwitz*, 257–58.

9   www.collections.ushmm.org/search/catalog/irn516325.
10 www.collections.ushmm.org/search/catalog/irn50931.
11 www.collections.ushmm.org/search/catalog/irn505802.
12 www.collections.ushmm.org/search/catalog/irn504778.
13 Louis Brandsdorfer, *The Bleeding Sky*, 100–101.
14 Ibid., 101.

Chapter 25

1   Megargee, *The United States Holocaust Memorial Museum Encyclopedia of Camps and Ghettos, 1933–1945*, vol. 1, 668–69.
2   Ibid., 669.
3   Ibid.
4   Ibid.
5   Ibid.

Chapter 26

1   www.collections.ushmm.org.searchcatalog/irn50931.
2   Ibid.
3   Wanda Poltawska, *And I Am Afraid of My Dreams* (Hippocrene, 1989), 158.
4   Rivka Mincberg Greenberg, "My Journey through the Valley of the Shadow of Death," in Christopher R. Browning, *Remembering Survival: Inside a Nazi Slave-Labor Camp* (W.W. Norton, 2011).
5   Dan Stone, *The Liberation of the Camps: The End of the Holocaust and Its Aftermath* (Yale, 2015), 55.
6   www.collections.ushmm.org/search/catalog/irn516325.
7   www.collections.ushmm.org/search/catalog/irn50931.
8   Saidel, *The Jewish Women of Ravensbruck*, 155.
9   www.collections.ushmm.org/search/catalog/vha/15035.
10 Hedgepeth and Saidel, *Sexual Violence against Jewish Women during the Holocaust* (Brandeis Univ. Press, 2010), 18.
11 www.collections.ushmm.org/search/catalog/vha15035.
12 Morrison, *Ravensbrück: Everyday Life in a Women's Concentration Camp 1938–1945*, 304.

Chapter 27

1 www.collections.ushmm.org/search/catalog/irn/50931.

Chapter 28

1 Author conversation with Sarah Pass, May 2017.

Chapter 29

1 www.ushmm.org/wlc/en/article.php?ModuleId=10007306.

Chapter 30

1 Center of Military History (US Army), *A Brief History of the US Army in World War II: Campaigns of World War II* (2005), 25.
2 Micheal Clodfelter, *Warfare and Armed Conflicts: A Statistical Encyclopedia of Casualty and Other Figures, 1492–2015* (McFarland, 2017), 464.
3 Anonymous, *A Woman in Berlin: Eight Weeks in the Conquered City: A Diary* (Picador, 2017), 3.
4 Ibid., xix.

Chapter 31

1 www.yadvashem.org/yv/en/education/newsletter/33/anti_jewish.asp.
2 David Engel, "Patterns of Anti-Jewish Violence in Poland, 1944–1946," in *Yad Vashem Studies,* vol. XXVI (Yad Vashem, 1998).
3 Jan T. Gross, *Fear: Anti-Semitism in Poland after Auschwitz* (Random House, 2006), 81–117.
4 www.ushmm.org/wlc/en/article.php?ModuleId=10007941.

Chapter 32

1 www.ushmm.org/wlc/en/article.php?ModuleId=10005462.
2 Patt and Berkowitz, *We Are Here: New Approaches to Jewish Displaced Persons in Postwar Germany,* 181–84.
3 Ibid.

4   Brenner, *After the Holocaust*, 94.
5   Konigseder and Wetzel, *Waiting for Hope: Jewish Displaced Persons in Post-World War II Germany*, 132.
6   Brenner, *After the Holocaust*, 94.

Chapter 33

1   Angelika Konigseder and Juliane Wetzel, *Waiting for Hope: Jewish Displaced Persons in Post-World War II Germany* (Northwestern, 2001), 16.
2   Ibid., 6.
3   Avinoam J. Patt and Michael Berkowitz, eds., *We Are Here: New Approaches to Jewish Displaced Persons in Postwar Germany* (Wayne State, 2010), 211.
4   Michael Brenner, *After the Holocaust: Rebuilding Lives in Postwar Germany* (Princeton, 1999), 16.
5   Ibid., 13.
6   Brenner, *After the Holocaust: Rebuilding Lives in Postwar Germany*, 92.
7   Patt and Berkowitz, *We Are Here: New Approaches to Jewish Displaced Persons in Postwar Germany*, 123.
8   Ibid., 214.
9   Ibid., 109.

Chapter 36

1   A. W. Artenstein, "Influenza," in *Vaccines: A Biography*, 191–205.

Hyman and Sarah at my Bar Mitzvah (November 5, 1966). Hyman was my godfather and grew up in Plonsk with my dad. Sarah was my mom's second cousin, her closest living relative, and like an aunt to him.

My brother Herb's Bar Mitzvah (February 1973)

Sam and Helen at my Bar Mitzvah (November 5, 1966)

Helen's mother and grandparents

Sam Bagel's citizenship document (1954)

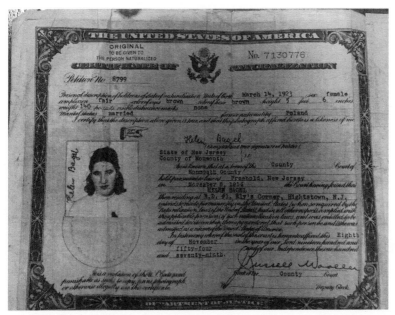

Helen Bagel's citizenship document (1954)

Sam and Helen packing eggs (1976)

Rick and Bridget Bagel, grandchildren of Sam and Helen (1998)

Sam & Ilana Bagel , Herb's children
Grandchildren of Sam & Helen Bagel

Sam Bagel singing klezmer at his seventieth birthday party

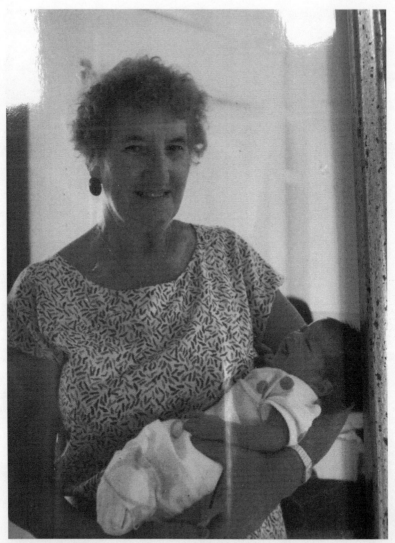

Helen with Bridget Bagel (born June 6, 1989)

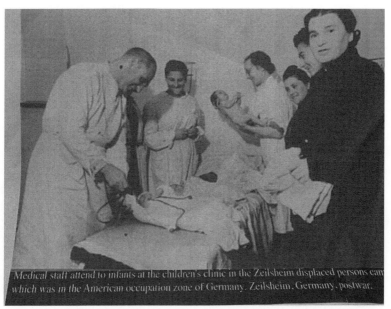

Medical staff attend to infants at the children's clinic in the Zeilsheim displaced persons camp which was in the American occupation zone of Germany. Zeilsheim, Germany, postwar.

The birth of my cousin Florence in May 1946, one of the first postwar Jewish babies born in Zalzeim. Her mom, Devorah (my dad's first cousin and sister to Meyer and Shlomo Fox), stands in the foreground.

My cousin Florence, who was in the birthing picture, hugging my mom (1977).